Empowered Leaders

Empowered Leaders provides educators with a practical guide for incorporating critical social justice themes into enrichment programming for gifted students in grades 4–5.

Featuring options for differentiation, digital learning, and talent development, each chapter offers detailed lesson plans and activities based around grade level themes that build as the students progress through middle school. Accessible and reader-friendly, lessons are student-centered and designed to foster globally conscious thought, empathetic discourse, and sustainable problem-solving skills.

Ideal for individual, co-teaching, or small group programs, this helpful resource equips teachers with the tools to incorporate social justice into any subject or classroom.

Bryan Kirby (@MrBKirby) and **Jessica Stargardter** (@MsStargardter) are gifted educators who graduated from the University of Connecticut. Bryan is currently a middle school gifted and talented teacher and Jessica is a Fulbright Scholar studying the education system in Finland. They are passionate about social justice education, technology integration, and equity in gifted programs. Bryan specializes in theater and science, while Jessica focuses on history and language arts.

Empowered Leaders

A Social Justice Curriculum for Gifted Learners, Grades 4–5

Bryan Kirby and Jessica Stargardter

Taylor & Francis Group

NEW YORK AND LONDON

Cover image: Designed by Jon Hull

First published 2022
by Routledge
605 Third Avenue, New York, NY 10158

and by Routledge
4 Park Square, Milton Park, Abingdon, Oxon, OX14 4RN

Routledge is an imprint of the Taylor & Francis Group, an informa business

© 2022 Taylor & Francis

The right of Bryan Kirby and Jessica Stargardter to be identified as authors of this work has been asserted in accordance with sections 77 and 78 of the Copyright, Designs and Patents Act 1988.

All rights reserved. The purchase of this copyright material confers the right on the purchasing institution to photocopy or download pages which bear either the photocopy or support material icon and a copyright line at the bottom of the page. No other parts of this book may be reprinted or reproduced or utilised in any form or by any electronic, mechanical, or other means, now known or hereafter invented, including photocopying and recording, or in any information storage or retrieval system, without permission in writing from the publishers.

Trademark notice: Product or corporate names may be trademarks or registered trademarks, and are used only for identification and explanation without intent to infringe.

Library of Congress Cataloging-in-Publication Data
A catalog record for this title has been requested

ISBN: 978-1-032-21911-0 (hbk)
ISBN: 978-1-032-21897-7 (pbk)
ISBN: 978-1-003-27053-9 (ebk)

DOI: 10.4324/9781003270539

Typeset in Palatino
by Deanta Global Publishing Services, Chennai, India

Access the Support Material: www.routledge.com/9781032218977

Contents

Foreword vi
Joseph S. Renzulli, Ed.D.
Acknowledgements viii
Author's Note ix

1 Cultivating a Social Justice Mindset in Gifted Learners 1

2 Laying the Foundation: The Schoolwide Enrichment Model 13

3 How to Teach Social Justice in a Schoolwide Enrichment Model ... 23

4 Identity 31

5 Empathy 63

Afterword 95
Lori Leibowitz
Appendix A 97
Appendix B 98
Appendix C 99
Appendix D 100
Appendix E 101
Appendix F 102
Appendix G 103
Appendix H 104

■ Foreword

Joseph S. Renzulli, Ed.D.

The principal goal of gifted education is to develop young people that have the investigative and creative capabilities to do good things that will make the world a better place. *Empowered Leaders: A Social Justice Curriculum for Gifted Learners, Grades 4–5* provides an inductive, investigative, and inquiry-based approach for pursuing this goal. The book focuses on *applying* knowledge-of and knowledge-how to real-world problems and situations in ways that model the *modus operandi* of the practicing professional, even if at a more junior level than that of adult experts. This approach increases collaboration, cooperation, the development of thinking skills and creativity, the construction of models, scientific and artistic contributions, and most importantly, developing the strategies for taking action to address social justice issues.

These kinds of introspective and exploratory skills are the things we should be using to increase society's reservoir of young people who are interested in fairness, equality, empathy for others, and even worldwide issues such as climate change, poverty, and pollution. These skills cannot be measured as precisely as math and reading test scores, they are the things that count when it comes to developing creative and productive contributions to one's school, community, or other target groups. Talent development opportunities in these areas should be available to all students; and it is for this reason that our Schoolwide Enrichment Model (Renzulli & Reis, 1991, 2014) casts a wide net that extends talent potential assessment beyond simply setting an arbitrarily established cut off score on an IQ test.

The skills mentioned above cannot be developed through the sit-memorize-and-repeat teaching approach that improves the standardized test scores most researchers use as the major dependent variables in their studies. Rather, an inductive and investigative pedagogy teaches young people how to find and focus a problem in which they have developed an interest and to apply investigative methodologies and creative thinking skills to challenging and exploratory endeavors. Expert advice from adults, how-to books, and virtually unlimited Internet tools can provide just-in-time information for the necessary resources about which students must gain guidance from their teachers. And like practicing professionals, students must explore various product formats and potential audiences for their final products, performances, presentations, and other modes of communication.

If we are going to evaluate and pass judgment on the importance and value of education programs that promote these skills, we must first and foremost examine the main purpose of these programs, which, as mentioned above, is to increase the world's reservoir of creative and productive people. A good model for this brand of evaluation might be the ways in which we look at the quality of medical school graduates, or conservatories that prepare our artists and performers. We look at the problems that they identify and the various options for addressing these problems. This is exactly what the authors of this book have done in creating a very realistic and practical set of activities for addressing social justice issues.

Joseph S. Renzulli, Ed.D.

References

Renzulli, J. S., & Reis, S. M. (1991). The schoolwide enrichment model: A comprehensive plan for the development of creative productivity. In N. Colangelo & G. A. Davis (Eds.), *Handbook of gifted education* (pp. 111–141). Allyn and Bacon.

Renzulli, J. S., & Reis, S. M. (2014). *The schoolwide enrichment model: A how-to guide for talent development.* (3rd ed.) Prufrock Press.

Acknowledgements

There are a number of people who have offered their guidance to us while writing this book. First, we would like to thank Joe and Sally for not only creating the bedrock for which this book stands, but for mentoring us throughout this process. When our prospectus was approved, the first meeting we set up, even before we met with the editorial team, was with them. We couldn't have done it without you.

We would also like to thank Lori Leibowitz, our friend and leader. Without you, we would have never submitted this book for publication. Thank you for pushing us to be better teachers, authors, and people.

We would also like to thank the amazing team of gifted & talented teachers that we work with: Alyssa, Anna, David, Jen, Jenn, Laura, Maria, Nicki, and Nicole.

Jay and Riley, thank you for keeping us honest and grounded.

Dr. Del Siegle, Dr. E. Jean Gubbins, Dr. Robin Hands, Dr. Marcia Gentry, Dr. Donna Ford, Dr. Joy Lawson Davis, Dr. James Kaufman, and so many others, thank you for inspiring us to be better educators, researchers, and writers. And thank you to Dr. Kaufman, Dr. Ronald Beghetto, and Brian Housand for letting us use their work in the text. A special thank you to Alexa Sorden and the team at Concourse Village Elementary School in Bronx, NY for coming up with TAG feedback and letting us use it in our book.

Janine and Julianna, thank you for reviewing our work and providing open and honest feedback about our writing.

Jon, Rishi, Jess, and Heather, thank you for providing immense support throughout this process. You were always there for us!

And to our families, thank you for supporting us as we became the people we are today.

We appreciate all of you!

Author's Note

Before we begin our journey together, we would like to acknowledge our privilege. We are two white, able-bodied, cis educators from a wealthy state in America. We are not experts in social justice education, but we are continually working towards becoming anti-racist and anti-bias educators. We understand that there is always more to learn. We hope to share our lessons with you so that you can adapt them to your student body, your school and district, and your geographic location.

At the time of publishing, the Connecticut State Department of Education, in a joint statement with multiple other state education associations, stands firm on its commitment to multicultural education. This joint statement argues that "our students are best served when empowered with the tools to understand and investigate the countless lived experiences that exist in the world around them" (2021). Not all teachers have the government's support to enact a social justice model in their classroom, so this type of curriculum may be controversial. We kept that in mind when writing this book.

These lessons have high levels of student-based inquiry, which should allow for flexibility to get around those who argue against social justice teaching. For example, students can pick any topic they choose for the Theme Project, as long as it relates to the grade level theme. In our classrooms, we supplement these lessons with weeks' worth of discussions around identity, gender, race, and privilege. We build a space in our classrooms where our students work with each other to discuss and understand the importance of an inclusive and supportive environment.

Teaching our students with a focus on social justice, infusing choice, and implementing project-based learning has been a journey for us. We strive each year to make our work better, more personalized, and more relevant for our students. We encourage you to use this book as a starting point and to adapt these ideas to what best fits your students' needs.

All of the information in this book is research-based and meant to support both students of color and white students. We believe that this work is for all students. No matter the make-up of your student population, this book is for you.

A Note on the Terms: Diversity, Inclusion, Multiculturalism, Anti-racism, Equity….

While the trending words change constantly, the importance of the work does not. The murders of George Floyd, Breonna Taylor, and Ahmaud Arbery may have started a racial awakening for many white people. Black and Brown people have been fighting for justice long before the summer of 2020.

As white educators, we recognize that so many systems in education are rooted in white supremacy. We planned this curriculum to connect children to their identities while also encouraging them to recognize the diversity of others. Our hope is to continue to push the world of gifted education towards justice and equity for all.

We aimed to use words that state exactly what we mean. As the world continually changes, our words may grow out of date, but our intentions to teach students to think critically about the world around them hopefully will not. We know a focus on teaching and learning through a social justice lens will help to raise a new and open-minded generation of leaders. Students have the potential to change the world. It is important that educators provide students with the opportunity to do so. Empowerment is not about defining how the students succeed, it is getting out of their way so that they can research and then rise up against unjust systems. Gifted students grow up to become local, national, and global leaders; let's work to ensure that our future leaders are both empathetic and empowered in their fight for justice.

A Note on the Resources

All of the resources printed in this book are also available online at the publisher's website in PDF form. For more information and printable copies, please visit www.routledge.com/9781032218960.

Reference

Connecticut State Department of Education, Connecticut Association of Public School Superintendents, Connecticut Association of Boards of Education, Connecticut Association of Schools, American Federation of Teachers Connecticut, & Connecticut Education Association. (2021, July 14). Joint statement on the importance of a culturally responsive education [Press Release]. https://portal.ct.gov/SDE/Press-Room/Press-Releases/2021/Joint-Statement-on-the-Importance-of-a-Culturally-Responsive-Education

Chapter 1

Cultivating a Social Justice Mindset in Gifted Learners

Social Justice Education

The term "social justice" is thrown around a lot nowadays. It's molded and squeezed to fit into companies' mission statements and people's Instagram captions. Its buzzword status waters down the meaning and can evoke groans in people who take true action against injustice. This chapter is about ironing out the trendy nature of this phrase and urging real action in its place. We will outline the need for more social justice focused classrooms for gifted learners, as well as the logistics of incorporating this mindset into your instruction. *Empowered Leaders* is about fighting for educational equity for all students with gifts and talents by cultivating a social justice mindset.

For some teachers, infusing social justice into classroom lessons can be daunting, overwhelming, and sometimes even looked down upon by administrators and/or families. Other teachers have been discussing these topics for many years, navigating the obstacles and successes as they come. We hope you can use this book, no matter where you are in your journey of creating a social justice focused classroom.

According to the United Nations, "social justice is an underlying principle for peaceful and prosperous coexistence within and among nations. We advance social justice when we remove barriers that people face because of gender, age, race, ethnicity, religion, culture or disability" (2020). The United Nations' pursuit of social justice is at the core of every decision they make in carrying out their mission. The same should be true for every decision an educator makes in their classroom or in their school district at large.

Social Justice in education is "both a process and a goal". The end goal is "full and equal participation of all groups in a society that is mutually shaped to meet their needs" (Bell, 1997, p. 3). It is a commitment to challenge inequalities based on power and privilege. This curriculum can be part of your process and goal for creating more equitable gifted programs and providing opportunities for your students to engage in discussions and projects about the world around them.

Topics taught in a social justice focused classroom may include race and racism, gender identity, class, privilege, climate change, human rights, and the list goes on. However, it is not only about the topics. Social justice education is about the mindset educators cultivate in their students. With all the content knowledge in the world, students still need to be taught the critical thinking skills that go along with becoming collaborative, open-minded, justice-seeking citizens. We hope to not only empower future leaders, but

DOI: 10.4324/9781003270539-1

to also empower current teachers to rethink the education of gifted learners through a social justice lens.

A Social Justice Lens

Empowered Leaders is a curriculum for gifted learners with a focus on social justice. This lens can be applied to any content area or curriculum. It can be applied to any set of standards and any classroom setting.

This lens is important because gifted learners grow up to be in positions of power (See Chapter 2). There are a few ways in which this impending power makes a social justice mindset and curriculum important. Those identified as "gifted" in K–12 education are disproportionately white. This disproportionality is also apparent in the leadership of our major companies, political parties, and government systems. If white students grow up to be top earners, leading groups of people, it is imperative that they also can use their privilege to fight unjust systems. Therefore, teaching white students the importance of social justice is extremely important (Ford, 2011; Kleinrock, 2021). *Empowered Leaders* is the framework to begin cultivating a social justice mindset in these future leaders.

Just as we want white students to grow up to dismantle systems that perpetuate injustice, we recognize the inequities within the system of gifted programs that prevent students of color from being in these programs. *Empowered Leaders* hopes to tackle disproportionality in gifted programs by empowering teachers to spot the talent in students of color, multilingual learners, Twice Exceptional (2e) learners, and students from low-income communities. By providing a structured, rigorous curriculum that holds a mirror to potentially gifted students, we hope that general education teachers will have a clearer opportunity to identify students.

Incorporation of Social Justice Education

Across the nation, there are many ways students with gifts and talents are serviced. Not only are there different definitions labeling our students state to state, but there are also different mandates, laws, identification protocols, programs, and curricula. It can be difficult to discern what is best practice. The key to a good curriculum for the gifted is to be flexible in its application. We hope you can implement this curriculum no matter what your services look like.

Here are a couple of situations in which social justice education can be incorporated into your school or classroom effectively.

Homogenous Group Setting

For school districts that encourage pull-out services, cluster grouping, or homogenous grouping for gifted learners, social justice education could be extremely beneficial. If you are working with a group of only gifted learners, you can focus your teaching completely on social justice education. While you may still have variation in your group that requires differentiation, you may not need as many scaffolds for your students to access the content. Your group may also have more background information in terms of academic vocabulary, research skills, and content-specific knowledge. This can be beneficial to you as a teacher because you can engage your students in deeper conversations and more rigorous application of knowledge and higher order thinking.

For example, if you are incorporating the topic of climate change into your lessons, a homogenous group of gifted learners may already have a basic understanding of climate change. You may be able to skip more introductory information on the topic and dive deeper into how climate change disproportionately affects low-income communities and communities of color. You may be able to have a Socratic Seminar (see Chapter 3) on the effects of fracking on indigenous populations in the United States. An in-person or digital discussion with a young climate activist may also bring the real-world spark to your classroom. All these examples would be beneficial to all populations of students, but the pace at which teachers can implement these exercises can be faster with a group of gifted learners. There can also be a stronger emphasis on intersectional and critical thinking and independent or collaborative research.

Heterogenous Group Setting

Other gifted services may include co-teaching or a single teacher differentiating across multiple ability levels. In a classroom with a wide range of learners, teaching social justice topics is still possible, and encouraged. The *Empowered Leaders* curriculum can be implemented just as effectively in a classroom of mixed abilities. By removing scaffolds for gifted learners, those students may be able to work quickly through information they have already mastered and move towards extension activities that may include project-based learning, choice boards, researching, or interacting with guest speakers or community mentors.

For example, a teacher can decide to do a unit on immigrants' rights with a focus on lessons incorporating the Enrichment Triad Model (See Chapter 2). Gifted learners in the class may be able to work on finding immigrant advocacy groups in the community to contact while other students are learning content knowledge.

With a mixed group, teachers can also add scaffolds to the *Empowered Leaders* curriculum to service general education and special education students as well.

Afterschool Setting

The *Empowered Leaders* resources can make for great enrichment experiences or afterschool groups. Students who self-select to be in a group focused on social justice are more engaged and motivated by the activities. The curriculum can be implemented on a weekly basis, culminating in a community service project or presentation of research to an authentic audience, or people who would truly be impacted by the project. An example of this would be, if the students are focused on recycling in schools, it is no use to present to the class since the students have little power to change the recycling process on their own in the school. Instead, students can present to the principal, the board of education, or a local recycling group that focuses on getting recycle bins into schools. The lessons provided in the following chapters can easily be implemented afterschool and adapted to an enrichment setting.

Enrichment Clusters

A school structure that can be implemented as part of the Schoolwide Enrichment Model is called Enrichment Clusters (see Chapter 2). This structure follows the Enrichment Learning and Teaching aspect of the model. Enrichment Clusters are short courses based on student interest and choice. They are provided schoolwide as an opportunity for all learners to engage in enrichment learning. The implementation of Enrichment Clusters is also a way to identify students with talent. Clusters allow teachers to see students motivated and excited about learning because the course is on a topic based on student choice. For example, some cluster topics might be about space, quilting, environmental justice, or yoga and meditation. An enrichment cluster might be the perfect time and place to incorporate the *Empowered Leaders* curriculum at your school.

Across General Education Content Areas

Social justice education is not just for English and Social Studies teachers. Social justice topics can be incorporated across all content areas. It is not only possible to do this, but also crucial. Students need to learn that social justice is important to all fields of study. As students grow up to become empowered leaders, they will enter into a diverse set of careers. Scientists, artists, mathematicians, actors, musicians, construction workers, to name a few, all benefit from looking at their job through a social justice lens. It is not just for writers and politicians. Teachers have a responsibility to teach students through this lens in all content areas.

We have compiled a list of ways to incorporate social justice topics into your lessons by content area and grade level theme. The possibilities are endless, and the list is just the beginning.

Table 1.1 Social justice topics by content area and grade level theme

	IDENTITY	**EMPATHY**
ENGLISH	*A Kids Book About Identity* By Jimmy Gomez	*A Kids Book About Empathy* By Daron Roberts
MATH	Graph of personal hobbies & interests	Student designed poll or survey of their Peers
SCIENCE	*Who, Me? A Scientist* By Learning for Justice	Gender & Racial Breakdown of STEM Careers
SOCIAL STUDIES	Individualism vs. Collectivism	*Strictly No Elephants* By Lisa Mantchev
ARTS & MUSIC	Self Portraits	Your Name is a Song By Jamilah Thompkins-Bigelow
DIGITAL LITERACY	Personal Online Presence	Cyberbullying

Social Justice Education for All

Just as social justice education can be incorporated into every content area, it can also be taught to every student. While we are focusing on gifted learners for the purpose of this book, we recognize that all students would benefit from this curriculum.

Multilingual Learners

Students who speak multiple languages should be celebrated in our schools. However, traditionally, Multilingual Learners (MLLs) are underrepresented in gifted programs. This does not mean that MLLs do not have potential or talent. This means that our gifted programs are not designed to effectively identify and/or service MLLs. Teaching social justice topics may be a great way to spot talent in MLLs and in turn, identify or service appropriately. Like multicultural education, by integrating social justice education, students can see themselves and their communities in the curriculum and take direct action to help people they know. This increase in interest and passion will lead to more students showing talent, including MLL students.

Twice-Exceptional Learners

Students who have a diagnosed disability and have been identified as gifted are labeled Twice-Exceptional (2e). 2e learners are also underrepresented in gifted programs, often because one label overshadows the other. For example, a student with Attention Deficit Hyperactivity Disorder (ADHD) may not be recommended for a gifted program because they demonstrate little task commitment since their ADHD prevents them from being able to focus on small tasks such as completing a worksheet. Despite this, they are highly capable of understanding the content and may flourish during interest-based learning. 2e learners can benefit from learning about social justice topics because they may be more engaged in interest-or real-world project-based learning. Just as with MLLs, social justice topics can be more engaging to 2e learners, allowing teachers to spot talent more easily.

Getting Started

We often get asked, "I understand why social justice is so important, but where do I start?" This is a great question. We will outline a few steps to take before incorporating a social justice mindset into your classroom, school, or district programming.

Administration

Everyone has someone they answer to. Whether you are a teacher and you answer to building level administration such as an assistant principal and principal or if you are a principal and you answer to the superintendent, it is important to understand your administrator's stance on teaching social justice. We have had our own experiences with many administrators, ranging from aware and supportive to racist and combative. *Empowered Leaders* hopes to guide the incorporation of social justice education into learning for gifted learners. Use this book as a framework to show your administrators that social justice curriculum can be beneficial to gifted learners.

Our advice is to use facts and research to back up all instructional decisions. If your superior claims that social justice is too political, remind them that teaching with a social justice lens is about fostering peace and recognizing humanity. It is not about pushing a political agenda or viewpoint. This curriculum emphasizes choice, a quality that we argue is important in social justice education. The goal is to allow students to be curious and to learn about social justice topics in a safe, educational setting.

Families & Community Members

It is important to be transparent with students' families. Incorporating social justice topics into lessons can bring about discussions that may be considered taboo, controversial or even inappropriate by students' families. While we do not recommend asking for permission, we always let our parents and families know about the upcoming topics prior to starting a lesson or unit. A simple letter or email home can make a huge difference. Emphasize that when teaching social justice topics, students are being asked to analyze the facts and come to their own conclusions. It is not about valuing one personal viewpoint over another. The why of teaching social justice topics is very important for parents and families to understand. In our experience, with this preemptive communication, schools and teachers will get less pushback.

BOX 1.1: SAMPLE LETTER FOR PARENTS & FAMILIES

Dear Parent or Guardian,

We are excited to begin a new unit of instruction with challenging texts and multimedia sources. Students will be learning about informational text through the topic of school safety and gun control. We hope to bring in guest speakers and provide a relevant and important look at a difficult topic.

School safety and gun control is a topic near and dear to our hearts. While we both feel safe coming to school each and every day, we are aware of the pattern of violence in schools happening in the last decade. We are also aware of the growing anxiety students face when coming to school. We hope this upcoming unit will provide students with the language to express their thoughts and the knowledge to formulate their own opinions.

This unit aligns with Common Core State Standards while also pushing students outside of the regular curriculum. Students will be asked to write a research article and present it to an authentic audience. We, as their teachers, will become facilitators in their learning while students will decide the path they hope to take with their research.

> We will follow closely the guidelines put forth by the National Association of School Psychologists. We have attached those guidelines for you to read. If you see your student needs someone to talk to, please let us know. Our school has a variety of mental health support within the building.
>
> Please reach out if you have any questions or concerns.

Encourage a partnership between your school or classroom and families and community members. Oftentimes, inviting community members into the school can be beneficial when teaching social justice topics. With technology, guest speakers can visit in-person, virtually, or even record themselves to be played asynchronously. The community available to students can become larger than their drivable geographic region because of many technological advancements. Invite guest speakers from around the world into your school or classroom. Be mindful of the voices you are inviting into your classroom. Just as you are encouraging your students to recognize and celebrate diversity, you should as well in your guest speakers. Do your best to compensate speakers for their time; sometimes administrators are willing to cover this cost. Oftentimes, all it takes is a simple email ask for a professor, doctor, lawyer, activist, or organizer to say yes to visiting your students.

> **BOX 1.2: SAMPLE GUEST SPEAKER INVITATION**
>
> Dear Human Rights Lawyer,
>
> In Gifted & Talented this year, we are investigating social justice issues based on student choice and interest. Students are empowered to ask questions about real-world issues. Grade 6 students are exploring a variety of topics in the hopes of making meaningful change in their community.
>
> The students are studying human rights by investigating human rights violations in the immigration and deportation process. So far, they have conducted research to gain a better understanding of the process. They are curious to learn more about this topic from you because of your personal and professional experiences with immigration.
>
> As an expert in the field of human rights law, we would love to invite you to speak on this topic. You are welcome to our visit our classroom virtually or in-person depending on what's best for you.
>
> If you are interested, please let me know.

A template of this letter is available in Appendix A.

Social Emotional Learning

Another big part of "Getting Started" is first recognizing the social emotional needs of students. Building relationships is our number one recommended first step in teaching social justice topics. Students need to feel comfortable in their classroom environment and with their teachers before engaging with these topics. But keep in mind the white supremacist thinking that comes into play with classic SEL and emotional regulation techniques. Validate the range of emotions students will display when learning about these topics. Remember that their cultural identities will partially dictate how they will respond, and that could differ from your own cultural response. The Communities for Just Schools Fund writes in *Medium* that "[a] culturally-affirming social-emotional learning relates students back to their ancestry while recognizing and addressing trauma" (2020). When working with a social justice classroom, we need to be fully aware of how ALL of our practices affect students. Our SEL curriculum and strategies also should be looked at through an equity lens. In our classroom, we engage students and families with periodic check-ins related to how they're feeling about the class, curriculum, and environment.

Classroom Environment

Just as social emotional learning and building relationships with students is crucial, so is the physical (or virtual) space where students learn. As teachers, it is our job to create an environment that nurtures and develops students' gifts. We should think about how our classroom supports these gifts, whether that be an updated library, access to technology to engage students' passions, or classroom decorations that match students' identities. This may seem expensive, and it can be. Look into crowdfunding and grants to makeover your classroom, ask your administration to buy you new furniture, or share an Amazon wish list with families, friends, and social media followers. One online store we use is Amplifier (www.amplifier.org); it has a lot of great art for your walls. Their mission is to "amplify the most important movements of our time". We also recommend looking into non-profit and local artists in your area, as well as having students design art to make the classroom a more community centered space. Even without all the new technology and flashy posters, the environment still needs to be considered. How are your desks arranged? Where do you spend your time? Where do your kids spend their time? We continually change our rooms throughout the year, including setting the desks up in pods and in a large circle, depending on the unit.

But on top of the physical environment, the learning environment is also important. This is very similar to what was discussed in the social and emotional setting above. The two concepts are highly interconnected. This section focuses on students' ability to discuss and debate the content, which should come after you create a socially rich environment. First, you need the students to feel like they're a part of the classroom, like it is their space as much as it is yours. We recommend that you create class charters, also known as community agreements or community ethos. This allows the students to have a say in how the classroom is run – to make it more of a democratic process. How you run the class is up to you, and it is not our place to tell you, but when starting to think about a liberatory classroom environment, we recommend reading "Building a Teaching Community" by bell hooks' from *Teaching to Transgress*. Though it discusses hooks' experience in a college level classroom, we argue that the underlying principals she reflects on work in all grades.

Personal and Professional Development

Reflection on personal identity, privileges, and perspectives is essential when developing and facilitating curriculum based on social justice topics. It is easy to perpetuate stereotypes, show only one perspective, or push personal cultural norms and practices on students who may not conform to those same ideals, especially if you yourself are part of the dominant culture. Educators need to reflect on personal biases before, during, and after engaging in social justice topics with students. There are many books, websites, groups, and social media accounts to engage with. As we noted earlier, social justice education is both a process and a goal. You are never done learning. After working for years on this work, we both still are reading and learning more – especially when it comes to teaching students with different social identities than us.

Elements of Social Justice Education

Themes

In *Empowered Leaders*, we use grade level themes to guide our instruction. Each grade level aligns all learning objectives and essential questions to a specific theme based on Learning for Justice's Social Justice Standards. The themes act as a focus for teachers and students. The themes build on each other as the students grow and mature throughout their elementary and middle school years. Adding a variety of perspectives and contexts over the years allows students to look at the themes from different lenses, building on their ability to understand each theme. If your programming is designed to allow for this, the themes can build from year to year. As a teacher, you can add on to the previous years' themes to provide more context and more depth. Below is a brief overview of the themes covered in this curriculum. For more in-depth explanation, please turn to the respective chapters.

Essential Components of High-Quality Curriculum

With social justice education, we argue that there are four essential components for a high-quality curriculum: Student-driven learning, inquiry-based learning, real-world investigations, and authentic audiences. Putting students at the center of their learning is important because oftentimes curriculum is white-washed, Eurocentric, and missing marginalized voices. Our students need to be able to recognize themselves in their learning. Student-driven learning ensures that students can look inward at their own identities or

Table 1.2 Identification of Grade Level Theme

Grade	4	5	6	7	8
Theme	Identity	Empathy	Diversity	Justice	Action

explore other identities they are curious about. Students should have control of the curriculum, ensuring that they will be learning based on interest.

Social justice education is most effective when students are asking questions. Just as they need to be at the center of their learning, they need to also be curious about the topic. By having students investigate and create their own questions, you are also allowing students to have agency while also pushing them to be more inquisitive about the world around them. This teaches students important thinking skills as well as giving them autonomy and agency. They are more engaged in learning when they can connect to the topic. Incorporating real world issues into lessons and units can make all the difference in motivating students to complete tasks and drive their learning. These don't have to be global problems like world hunger but can be specific to your school or town community. We always push students to start small, but with so many systemic issues around them, it is no doubt likely that students will jump for the flashy headline-grabbing topics first.

After all the work of investigating a real-world issue through student-driven, inquiry-based learning, students need to present their learning to an authentic audience. This could look like inviting community members or families to listen to presentations. Students could also present to administration or at a Board of Education meeting. Another example could be students presenting to younger grades about what they learned. This aspect is often ignored, but equally important as the others.

If you look carefully at the four components of a high-quality social justice curriculum, all push teachers to be "guides on the side", as we like to say. This is also an important aspect of the pedagogical model we use, Schoolwide Enrichment Model, described in the next chapter. We provide students with the tools to become the ones in charge. When presenting to an authentic audience, the students are not going to have the teacher changing the script in the moment, they are going to need to know how to adapt in the moment. This should be the same with learning. Educators need to provide students with what they need to engage with content, and then take a step back and become a facilitator to let the students drive their learning. This may be challenging to some, but we guarantee that it will be worthwhile in the end.

Additional Resources

There are many resources on teaching social justice topics to elementary students as well as personal and professional development for elementary school teachers. It can become overwhelming, so we've compiled a list of our favorites that have guided us on this journey.

BOX 1.3: SOCIAL JUSTICE EDUCATION RESOURCES

Books

The Anti-Racist Writing Workshop: How to Decolonize the Creative Classroom (2021) by Felicia Rose Chavez

Black Ants and Buddhists: Thinking Critically and Teaching Differently in the Primary Grades (2006) by Mary Cowhey

Cultivating Genius: An Equity Framework for Culturally and Historically Responsive Literacy (2020) by Gholdy Muhammad

Culturally Responsive Teaching & the Brain: Promoting Authentic Engagement and Rigor Among Culturally and Linguistically Diverse Students (2015) by Zaretta Hammond and Y. Jackson

For White Folks Who Teach in the Hood....and the Rest of Y'all Too: Reality Pedagogy and Urban Education (2016) by Christopher Emdin

Start Here, Start Now: A Guide to Antibias and Antiracist Work in Your School Community (2021) by Liz Kleinrock

Teaching for Black Lives (2018) edited by Dyan Watson, Jesse Hagopian, Wayne Au

Teaching to Transgress: Education as the Practice of Freedom (2003a) by bell hooks

Teaching Community: A Pedagogy of Hope (2003b) by bell hooks

Multicultural Gifted Education (2011) by Donna Y. Ford

Not Light, but Fire: How to Lead Meaningful Race Conversations in the Classroom (2018) by Matthew R. Kay

Start Seeing & Serving Underserved Gifted Students: 50 Strategies for Equity and Excellence (2020) by Jennifer Ritchotte, Chin-Wen Lee, and Amy Graefe

Websites

Abolitionist Teaching Network (https://abolitionistteachingnetwork.org)
Black Lives Matter at School (https://www.blacklivesmatteratschool.com)
Educators for Justice (https://educatorsforjustice.org)
Facing History & Ourselves (https://www.facinghistory.org/)
Learning for Justice (https://www.learningforjustice.org)
Teaching for Black Lives (https://www.teachingforblacklives.org)
The Center for Racial Justice in Education (https://centerracialjustice.org)

Social Media Accounts

@teachersforblacklives (Instagram)
@teachfortheculture (Instagram)
@theconsciouskid (Instagram)
@so.informed (Instagram)
@wokekindergarten (Instagram)

References

Bell, L. A. (1997). Theoretical foundations for social justice education. In M. Adams, L. A. Bell, & P. Griffin (Eds.), *Teaching for diversity and social justice: A sourcebook* (pp. 3–15). New York: Routledge.

Chavez, F. R. (2021). The anti-racist writing workshop. Haymarket Books.

Communities for Just Schools Fund. (2020, May 12). *When sel is used as another form of policing.* Medium. https://medium.com/@justschools/when-sel-is-used-as-another-form-of-policing-fa53cf85dce4.

Cowhey, M. (2006). *Black ants and Buddhists: Thinking critically and teaching differently in the primary grades.* Stenhouse Publishers.

Emdin, C. (2016). *For white folks who teach in the hood… and the rest of y'all too.* Beacon Press.

Ford, D. Y. (2011). *Multicultural gifted education.* (2nd ed.) Prufrock Press.

Hammond, Z., & Jackson, Y. (2015). *Culturally responsive teaching and the brain: Promoting authentic engagement and rigor among culturally and linguistically diverse students.* Corwin.

hooks, bell. (2003a). *Teaching to transgress: Education as the practice of freedom.* Routledge.

hooks, bell. (2003b). *Teaching community: A pedagogy of hope.* Routledge.

Kay, M. R. (2018). *Not light, but fire: How to lead meaningful race conversations in the classroom.* Stenhouse Publishers.

Kleinrock, L. (2021). *Start here, start now: A guide to antibias and antiracist work in your school community.* Heinemann.

Muhammad, G. (2020). *Cultivating genius: An equity framework for culturally and historically responsive literacy.* Scholastic.

Ritchotte, J. A., Lee, C.-W., & Graefe, A. K. (2020). *Start seeing & serving underserved gifted students: 50 strategies for equity and excellence.* Free Spirit Publishing.

United Nations. (2020). Closing the inequalities gap to achieve social justice. https://www.un.org/en/observances/social-justice-day

Watson, D., Hagopian, J., & Au, W. (Eds.). (2018). *Teaching for black lives.* Rethinking Schools.

Chapter 2

Laying the Foundation

The Schoolwide Enrichment Model

All Roads Lead to Rome.

That is how Dr. Joseph Renzulli and Dr. Sally Reis start off their invaluable guide to the Schoolwide Enrichment Model (SEM), the model that is the basis for our curriculum. Thinking about backwards design for lessons, we want students to be able to think independently and creatively about social issues that affect the world around them while also preparing them to take action on their own terms. And there are many ways to get to this point. This book outlines one of those ways. The next two chapters will lay the foundation for our curriculum, focusing on gifted theory in the first and multicultural education in the second.

The Schoolwide Enrichment Model

The Schoolwide Enrichment Model (SEM) is a flexible model of talent development for schools. By combining pre-existing school structures, like the regular curriculum and the continuum of special services, with gifted modifications, a strengths assessment, and the infusion of enrichment, SEM is a research-based program for any school. Ford (2011) states that the Schoolwide Enrichment model is also the most inclusive model for gifted education, focusing on talent development, supplementing challenge for those who might be more advanced than the standard curriculum.

In this chapter, we will define the four subtheories of the Schoolwide Enrichment Model, as they play an important role in the development of our curriculum. When originally conceptualizing this curriculum, we focused on the four subtheories as a basis for what we wanted the structure to focus on. For more information on the SEM topics not covered in this text, visit gifted.uconn.edu or purchase a copy of *The Schoolwide Enrichment Model: A How-to Guide for Talent Development* (2014) from Prufrock Press (Routledge).

Figure 2.1 The Schoolwide Enrichment Model. Republished with permission of Taylor & Francis Group LLC - Books, from *The Schoolwide Enrichment Model: A How-to Guide for Talent Development* by Joseph S. Renzulli & Sally Reis, 3rd edition, 2014]; permission conveyed through Copyright Clearance Center, Inc.

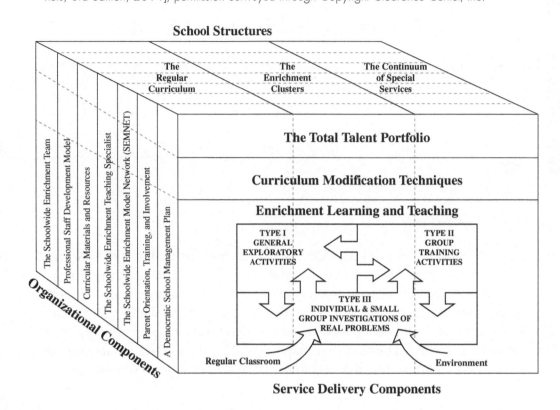

What are Gifted Behaviors?

Giftedness is a highly misunderstood term. There is an extreme divide between what researchers and what current educators view as giftedness, especially when it comes to students of color (Russell, 2018; Speirs Neumeister, et al., 2007). This is primarily due to lack of grade-specific training on giftedness for general education teachers. Let's define what it means to be gifted and identify some of the possible behaviors gifted students exhibit.

In the Three-Ring Conception of Giftedness, the first subtheory of SEM, the definition of giftedness goes beyond academic scores. Giftedness is defined as the overlap between three clusters of traits: above average— but not necessarily superior— ability, creativity, and task commitment (Reis & Peters, 2020; Renzulli & Reis, 2014).

Above average ability is measured by cognitive tests and achievement tests, as well as by student grades. Above average task commitment focuses on the non-intellective trait of motivation. When identifying students, task commitment can be unofficially determined by teacher reports as well as through classroom observations by the gifted specialist.

The creativity cluster is one of the more ambiguous sides of this model because of, again, the lack of training in recognizing creativity in students, especially students of color. Creativity is defined as "anything that is determined to be both original and task appropriate as defined

Figure 2.2 The Three-Ring Conception of Giftedness. Republished with permission of Taylor & Francis Group LLC - Books, from *The Schoolwide Enrichment Model: A How-to Guide for Talent Development* by Joseph S. Renzulli & Sally Reis, 3rd edition, 2014]; permission conveyed through Copyright Clearance Center, Inc.

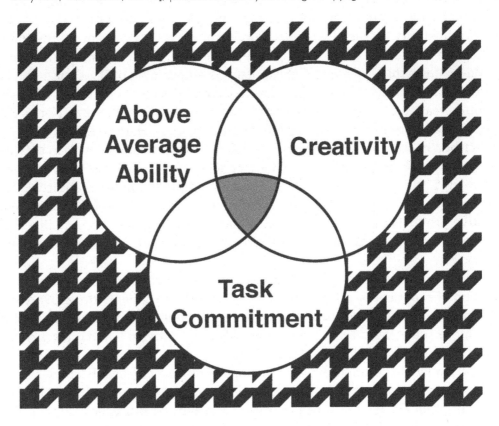

Figure 2.3 The Developmental Trajectory of Creativtiy. Classroom contexts for creativity, Ronald A. Beghetto & James C. Kaufman, *High Ability Studies*, copyright © European Council for High Ability, reprinted by permission of Taylor & Francis Ltd, http://www.tandfonline.com on behalf of European Council for High Ability.

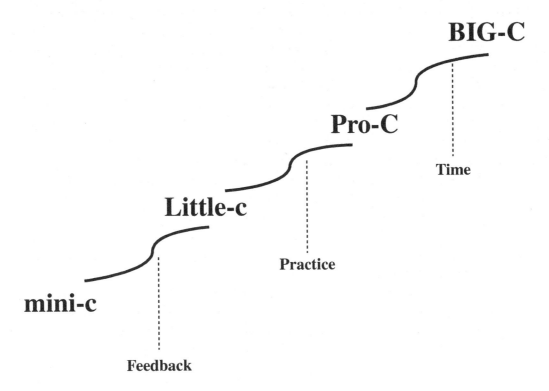

within a particular context" (Beghetto, 2013). Beghetto & Kaufman propose a Four-C Model of Creativity, defining the different levels of creativity that a person can achieve. This model elaborates on the previous research in creativity, which only included Big-C and little-c. These are the two levels of creativity that most people associate with creativity. Little-c is the everyday creativity we see in students. For example, when a student writes an ingenious poem in English class or has an interesting take on the Picasso Cubism assignment in art class, that is little-c. Meanwhile, Picasso's Cubism itself is an example of Big-C or a revolutionary large-scale act of creativity. Big-C is the most objective version of creativity. When we think of Steve Jobs' creation of the iPhone or Oscar Hammerstein II and Jerome Kern's *Show Boat*, there is no doubt in our minds that these revolutionary ideas were creative.

As described in Kaufman & Beghetto's model, there are transition levels in between Big-C and little-c. You don't just jump from elementary school art class to the Louvre overnight.

In between Little-c and Big-c is Pro-c. Pro-c is the professional creativity. Examples of Pro-C creativity are Christopher Doyle's cinematography and Beyoncé's songs. With time, these creative products can, and we would argue most likely will, become Big-C level. But we won't know until we look back years from now and reflect on the contribution of these artists to society.

The smallest level of creativity is mini-c, or the "novel and personally meaningful interpretation of experiences, actions, and events" (Kaufman & Beghetto, 2009). Mini-c is the creativity involved in learning that, with meaningful feedback, can leads to little-c. It also allows for more subjectivity than little-c does. Mini-c creativity is what teachers see daily. It is the combining of two colors of playdough in pre-school to create a new color or a high school music student experimenting with arrangements of a classical Bach piece.

Connecting this back to the Three-Ring Conception of Giftedness, the levels of creativity to look for in students are not those of Albert Einstein or Bill Gates (Big-C). But rather, teachers should focus on the mini-c and little-c levels of creativity. For example, if a student solves a math problem a different way than expected or attempts a different way of shading a drawing, that could be a novel way that they are thinking within the constraints of the assignment. Unfortunately, and more often than not, instead of being praised for their creativity, students are chastised for not following the prescribed method of learning. This is a mindset shift that we, as teachers, need to have when teaching and identifying potentially gifted students. Another way that a student can be creative is through everyday, or little-c, creativity (Kaufman & Beghetto, 2009). This is when students create a unique project for a book report or come up with an ingenious fix to a classroom issue. By reframing how to view creativity in the lens of mini-c and little-c creativity, teachers will find a much larger pool of creative students who could be potentially gifted.

It is important to note that students' traits do not always present equally like in Figure X. Students could be extremely creative, slightly above average in motivation and ability, and still be considered gifted. In most cases, students vary in their ability levels within each of the clusters, so it is important to stress this in identification protocols.

In using a broad definition of giftedness, we encompass learners who may not thrive in the traditional school environment, including populations of students who are historically underrepresented in gifted programs. We would argue that gifted education should be less about acceleration and more about development of these three clusters of behaviors, therefore focusing on creative productive giftedness, as opposed to academic giftedness. There is no doubt that students need to be challenged academically, but that doesn't mean we can't also provide them the opportunities to develop their talents and engage critically with the world

Figure 2.4 Depictions of the Three Clusters of Traits. Republished with permission of Taylor & Francis Group LLC - Books, from *The Schoolwide Enrichment Model: A How-to Guide for Talent Development* by Joseph S. Renzulli & Sally Reis, 2nd edition, 1997]; permission conveyed through Copyright Clearance Center, Inc.

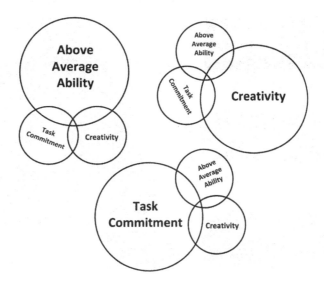

around them. "History does not remember persons who merely scored high on IQ tests and/or learned their lessons well" (Renzulli, 1982).

And when we look towards the measures to identify this type of giftedness, we need to expand beyond just assessments of learning such as standardized tests. We should be focusing on the potential students have to learn through formative measure. In this case, assessments for learning, like student completed assignments or experiences with enrichment activities, are more meaningful and can show the potential the student has to learn and succeed (Renzulli, 2020). By doing this, you are widening your talent pool to not just those students who do well on tests, but also those who are dedicated, creative individuals with talents. We hope to include students who love art and music, who love building and creating, who love coding and designing, and are above average in these passions.

The Enrichment Triad Model

How can teachers engage with talent spotting and creativity in a classroom while still adhering to the rigorous state and national standards. Is there even enough time? The main thing that we are asked as teachers when it comes to curriculum is to raise student achievement across the board and have data to back it up. When students enjoy and are engaged with what they're learning, when they have an enthusiasm for what they're learning, then high levels of achievement will come naturally. This is reflected in Renzulli's Three E Model: Engagement, Enjoyment, and Enthusiasm are the three E's required for student achievement (Renzulli & Reis, 2014).

The key to obtaining the three Es is by increasing student agency and choice in the curriculum. This is where the Enrichment Triad Model comes in. This model is a deductive, investigative-based approach to learning that focuses on three levels of enrichment: Type I, Type II, and Type III.

Figure 2.5 The Three Es. Republished with permission of Taylor & Francis Group LLC - Books, from *The Schoolwide Enrichment Model: A How-to Guide for Talent Development* by Joseph S. Renzulli & Sally Reis, 3rd edition, 2014]; permission conveyed through Copyright Clearance Center, Inc.

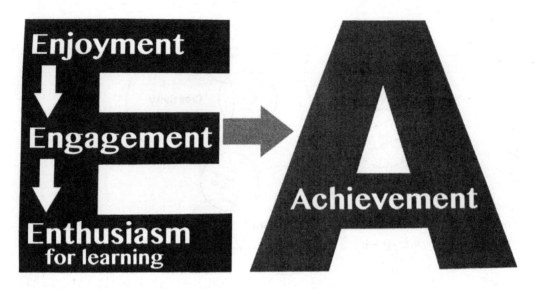

The first part of this model, Type I, is general exploratory activities. Teachers provide students with activities to get them interested in a topic, to spark their romance with the topic, as English philosopher A.N. Whitehead would put it. This can come in the form of a guest speaker, a documentary, a coding exercise, or even a short clip of something happening in the news. Some of the best ways that we've discovered for Type I enrichment are through choice boards, menus, and guest speakers, though there are many other roads you can take with Type Is.

Getting mentors and guest speakers may seem like a daunting task, but we have some suggestions on how to make it easier. One possible option is to reach out to grad students and professors at local colleges and universities, as well as retired members of the community. This is even easier to arrange now that most districts have access to video conferencing platforms like Zoom, Google Meet, or Microsoft Teams, to name a few. However, before reaching out past your school walls, look inwards at the families, staff, and community members that have a stake in the school already. This group of stakeholders is usually an untapped wealth of knowledge and resources. An easy way to track all of that information is to use The ASPIRE Survey, created by Dr. Mallory M. Bagwell, and Dr. Michele Femc-Bagwell. This survey can be done with parents and guardians on an open house or back-to-school night. Along with the survey, ASPIRE is also a database tool for teachers to implement in their school that allows them to identify the assets, skills, professions, interests, relationships, and environments (ASPIRE) of the stakeholders of the school. This will allow you to know what you have already in your school community. For more information on the ASPIRE survey, visit www.theaspiresurvey.com.

Once a student finds an interest, the goal is to then have them learn the skills to create an actionable product. This is called Type II Enrichment. These "individual and group training activities [teach] a variety of cognitive, meta-cognitive, methodological, and affective skills" (Renzulli & Reis, 2014). The most common form of a Type II skill already embedded in classrooms is research skills, including how to assess the credibility of a source, how to take notes, how to cite, and of course, how to use Google. But there are many other Type II skills. Some of the skills that we've helped facilitate with elementary schoolers in the past few years are how to sew, how to edit a video, how to 3D print, how to write an email, and how to cut things on a Cricut. Each individual or group project will have a new Type II skill to master, which may sound daunting. But you don't need to be an expert sewer to help facilitate a project where a student makes masks and donates them to the local homeless shelter. Thankfully, we live in a world with an abundance of resources, right at our fingertips. A quick Google video search turns up over 28 million results for "how to sew". Also, how-to books and video conferencing with community mentors are a great way to get Type II lessons into your classroom.

Once students are equipped with the skills, they can embark on a Type III project, a real-world investigation that culminates in an authentic product. Breaking that definition down, students start by taking their Type I interest and identifying a problem in their community related to that interest. They then research the problem, come up with a solution, and implement that solution, utilizing any Type II skills they learned along the way. Examples of this could be writing an op-ed for a paper, creating a presentation for the school board, raising money to redo the courtyard so students can use it, or even helping to reduce food waste in the school cafeteria.

A group of students in our district realized that the only graphic novels in the school were housed in the small school library, even though each teacher had their own in-classroom libraries. They decided that they were going to create a list of the student body's favorite graphic novel series and create a *Donors Choose* page so that they could infuse more graphic novels throughout the school.

We have seen firsthand just how rewarding and fun Type III projects are and how inspiring they could be; we wanted all of our students to complete a Type III project and to be students who continually want to make a positive change in their communities. However, especially in the beginning of our SEM journey, we weren't sure how to get them there. We needed something concrete to scaffold their experience, something halfway between a Type II and Type III. We needed a place for students to learn how to conduct effective research, a safe space to discuss social issues, and most importantly, a data-driven student-led project that could also act as a formative assessment for all the basic skills needed to complete a successful Type III project. And that is how this curriculum was born.

Research shows that many gifted learners grow up to be global leaders (Renzulli, 2002). Because of that, we like to infuse social justice into our Type III projects. We don't force students to choose a social justice topic for their Type III, but we provide them with the resources to understand the larger social context in which their problem lies. To do this, we must inspire students to think critically about the injustices in the world and to support and assist the activists fighting those injustices. For a reference sheet on the Enrichment Triad Model, see Appendix H.

That specifically is the focus of the final two subtheories of the Schoolwide Enrichment Model. Operation Houndstooth and Executive Functions: Leadership for a Changing World work together to push students to use their gifts for good in the world, to increase social capital through kind, empathetic, and effective leadership.

Operation Houndstooth

Operation Houndstooth discusses the interactions between six co-cognitive factors that help cognitive development.

Figure 2.6 Operation Houndstooth. Reprinted with permission of The National Research Center on the Gifted and Talented at the University of Connecticut.

OPERATION HOUNDSTOOTH

OPTIMISM	COURAGE	ROMANCE WITH A TOPIC OR DISCIPLINE
•hope •positive feelings from hard work	•Psychological/intellectual independence •moral conviction	•absorption •passion
SENSITIVITY TO HUMAN CONCERNS	PHYSICAL/MENTAL ENERGY	VISION/SENSE OF DESTINY
•insight •empathy	•charisma •curiosity	•sense of power to change things •sense of direction •pursuit of goals

WISDOM
SATISFYING LIFESTYLE
— diversity 差异性
— balance 平衡
— harmony 和谐
— proportion 比例

© Operation Houndstooth
The National Research Center on the Gifted and Talented
University of Connecticut
Joseph S. Renzulli, Rachel E. Sytsma, & Kristin B. Berman
November, 2000   www.gifted.uconn.edu

These factors are optimism, courage, romance with a topic or discipline, sensitivity to human concerns, physical/mental energy, and vision/sense of destiny. They also help students develop their sense of values, beliefs, and morality. This needs to be done gradually and throughout the student's schooling – it cannot be done just within the Type III project. That is why our curriculum focuses on a continual growth of student awareness in the social and political world around them. By emphasizing these six co-cognitive factors during discussions and research, students can build the awareness of how they impact the world and help to develop their own morality. Then when it is time to take action through their Type III project, they will understand the necessity to focus on diversity, balance, harmony, and proportion, as opposed to self-promotion and indulgences.

Executive Functions: Leadership for a Changing World

Executive Functions: Leadership for a Changing World is the final piece to Renzulli & Reis's Schoolwide Enrichment Model. This theory includes five non-cognitive abilities that gifted students need to realize in order to truly make a difference in the world, state, or community. These five factors are action orientation, social interactions, altruistic leadership, realistic self-assessment, and awareness of the needs of others (Renzulli & Reis, 2014). This is the glue that holds the entire Schoolwide Enrichment Model together.

Like Operation Houndstooth, these five executive functions aren't instilled in our students overnight; they need to be continually embraced and modeled. By starting off small and having students work at their own pace, we can assess where they are in understanding these terms and the significance of them, while continuing to model them in our own lives and work.

Why the Schoolwide Enrichment Model?

Currently, gifted programs across the country are plagued with underrepresentation and disproportionality (Callahan, 2005; Peters et al., 2021). The Schoolwide Enrichment Model is one way to start identifying talented students based on proportional representation of the population. The first step is to widen the talent pool, or group of students who can potentially receive gifted services, outside of just those who have had the opportunity to do well on metric scores. By looking at Assessment for Learning, like student completed tasks and experiences, as opposed to standardized Assessments of Learning, you will identify students who have fallen through the cracks for years before, especially those students who have high levels of co-cognitive factors like above-average task commitment and creativity (Renzulli, 2020). When students are given the opportunity to engage with topics that interest them, that they are passionate about, and create real change, they will flourish. Research shows that the Schoolwide Enrichment Model has been shown to reverse underachievement in all students, including those of underrepresented groups (Baum, Renzulli, & Hébert, 1999; Emerick, 1988). The basic idea surrounding this is the Three E Model. When students are engaged in what interests them, they tend to have higher achievement across the board. We hope that you can incorporate social justice teaching into any model of giftedness that your school or district uses. If you need a starting point to foster talent development in all students, we encourage you to take a deeper dive into the Schoolwide Enrichment Model.

References

Baum, S. M., Renzulli, J. S., & Hébert, T. P. (1999). Reversing underachievement: Creative productivity as a systematic intervention. *Gifted Child Quarterly, 39,* 224–235.

Beghetto, R. A. (2013). *Killing ideas softly: The promise and perils of creativity in the classroom.* Information Age Publishing.

Callahan, C. (2005). Identifying gifted students from underrepresented populations. *Theory into Practice, 44*(2), 98–104.

Emerick, L. (1988). Academic underachievement among the gifted: Students' perceptions of factors that reverse the pattern. *Gifted Child Quarterly, 36,* 140–146.

Ford, D. Y. (2011). *Multicultural gifted education.* (2nd ed.) Prufrock Press.

Kaufman, J. C., & Beghetto, R. A. (2009). Beyond big and little: The Four C Model of Creativity. *Review of General Psychology, 13*(1), 1–12. doi:10.1037/a0013688

Peters, P., Gubbins, E.J., Hamilton, R., McCoach, D.B., Siegle, D., & Puryear, J. (2021) Identifying Underrepresented Gifted Students: A Developmental Process. In: Smith, S.R. (ed.) *Handbook of Giftedness and Talent Development in the Asia-Pacific*. Springer International Handbooks of Education. Springer, Singapore. doi:10.1007/978-981-13-3041-4_21

Reis, S. M., & Peters, P. M. (2020). Research on the Schoolwide Enrichment Model: Four decades of insight, innovation, and evolution. *Gifted Education International*. doi:10.1177/0261429420963987

Renzulli, J. S. (1982). Dear Mr. and Mrs. Copernicus: We regret to inform you. *Gifted Child Quarterly, 26*(1), 11–14.

Renzulli, J. S. (1978). What makes giftedness? Re-examining a definition. Phi Delta Kappa, 60, 180–181.

Renzulli, J. S. (1990). A practical system for identifying gifted and talented students. *Early Child Development and Care, 63*(1), 9–18.

Renzulli, J. S. (2002). Expanding the conceptions of giftedness to include co-cognitive traits and to promote social capital. *Phi Delta Kappan, 84*(1), 33–58.

Renzulli, J. S. (2020, November 19). *Expanding student identification procedures by adding assessment for learning information*. Renzulli Center for Creativity Gifted Education and Talent Development. Retrieved May 8, 2021, from https://gifted.uconn.edu/schoolwide-enrichment-model/assessment_for_learning/.

Renzulli, J. S., & D'Souza, S. (2014). Intelligences outside the normal curve: Co-cognitive factors that contribute to the creation of social capital and leadership skills in young people. In Plucker, J. A., Callahan, C. M. (Eds.), Critical issues and practices in gifted education: What the research says (2nd ed., pp. 343–362). Prufrock Press.

Renzulli, J. S., & Reis, S. M. (1997). *The schoolwide enrichment model: A how-to guide for educational excellence* (2nd ed.). Creative Learning Press.

Renzulli, J. S., & Reis, S. M. (2014). *The schoolwide enrichment model: A how-to guide for talent development*. (3rd ed.) Prufrock Press.

Russell, J. L. (2018). High school teachers' perceptions of giftedness, gifted education, and talent development. *Journal of Advanced Academics, 29*(4), 275–303.

Speirs Neumeister, K. L., Adams, C. M., Pierce, R. L., Cassady, J. C., & Dixon, F. A. (2007). Fourth-grade teachers' perceptions of giftedness: Implications for identifying and serving diverse gifted students. *Journal for the education of the gifted, 30*(4), 479–499.

Chapter 3
How to Teach Social Justice in a Schoolwide Enrichment Model

When infusing social justice into your curriculum, it is important to reflect on to what extent you are doing it. James A. Banks, scholar of culturally responsive education, identified four levels for integrating multiculturalism into a curriculum: the contributions approach, the additive approach, the transformation approach, and the social action approach. In the contribution level of infusion, teachers add in holiday celebrations, and cultural touchpoints like food and dance, but never really commit to the actual infusion. These surface level additions come during certain times of year, or in response to a community or national event. The additive effect takes infusion a step further, adding in authors of color or different perspectives, without actually changing the structure of the curriculum or giving context to the addition. The contributions and additive approaches are basic and problematic (Scott, 2014).

The transformation approach to infusion restructures the curriculum to include authors of color, different perspectives, and events pertaining to other cultural groups. This restructuring takes a lot of work and constant professional development but allows students with marginalized identities to feel seen in the curriculum, like their ancestors' stories matter.

But we need to take it a step further. We should strive to reach Banks' Social Action approach to infusion of multiculturalism. Here students "identify important social problems and issues, gather pertinent data, clarify their values on the issues, make decisions, and take reflective actions to help resolve the issues or problem" (Ford, 2011). This is actually a very similar goal to Renzulli & Reis's Schoolwide Enrichment Model, with a multicultural lens. That is why we believe SEM and social justice education go together like peanut butter and jelly.

In other words, the Schoolwide Enrichment Model's focus on student-centered learning and real-world investigations connect perfectly to Bank's model of multicultural integration. When students have the autonomy to investigate problems they see in their world, like they do in a SEM school or program, they often demonstrate increased engagement and motivation, especially when compared to more traditional learning models. This flexibility allows for students to feel comfortable speaking their minds and engaging in topics that may be deemed "controversial". In addition, student-led investigations allow them to develop strong interests which tend to have a positive impact on them later in life (Reis & Peters, 2020). And when a topic is interesting, more students are likely to engage with it. That is one of the reasons why kids love to read *Stamped: Racism, Anti-racism, and You* by Jason Reynolds & Ibram X. Kendi. The authors open the book with a declaration to students, "Before we begin, let's get something straight. This is not a history book. I repeat, this is not a history book. At least not like the ones you're used to reading in school." The information in *Stamped* is presented in a clear and engaging way. This book is a perfect model for how all topics in school should be presented.

In this chapter, we provide standards, strategies, and tips for lesson design. Reading this chapter will set you up for the theme-based chapters to follow. This chapter can also be used to help you think about expanding this curriculum to support your students' interests in social justice. The purpose of the strategies provided is to not only increase student engagement, but also to get students feeling comfortable about discussing their personal opinions about social justice topics. We have used all of these in our classrooms before and have been amazed at the increased levels of engagement and participation. Within each section below, we will provide resources for you to use, as well as websites to help you find more information about the topics. As you and your students begin your journey into the grade level themes, we would highly encourage you to use some, if not all, of the below strategies to encourage individual student voices to be heard.

Standards

Standards are a tricky thing. We understand that currently all teachers must follow them, but the underlying principle of them causes us to think twice. Kleinrock writes that standards can marginalize some identities and we agree (2021, p. 77). Therefore, we will provide you with over-arching standards here, but only with careful thought and specificity regarding the creating organization and the use of the standard in our curriculum.

The National Association for Gifted Children also has K–12 Programming Standards that were considered when creating this curriculum.

BOX 3.1: NAGC K–12 PROGRAMMING STANDARDS

3.3.1. Educators develop and use curriculum that is responsive and relevant to diversity that connects to students' real-life experiences and communities and includes multiple voices and perspectives.

3.3.2. Educators encourage students to connect to others' experiences, examine their own perspectives and biases, and develop a critical consciousness.

3.3.3. Educators use high-quality, appropriately challenging materials that include multiple perspectives.

3.4.2. Educators provide opportunities for students with gifts and talents to explore, develop, or research in existing domain(s) of talent and/or in new areas of interest.

3.5.3. Educators scaffold independent research skills within students' domain(s) of talent.

4.3.1. Educators establish a safe and welcoming climate for addressing personal and social issues and give students a voice in shaping their learning environment.

4.4.2. Educators model appropriate language and strategies to effectively address issues such as stereotyping, bias, and discriminatory language and behaviors.

4.5.2. Educators provide resources that reflect the diversity of their student population to enhance oral, written, and artistic forms of communication.

(Professional Standards Committee)

Finally, the Common Core Standards that we followed were the College and Career Readiness standards. We find that, especially in a pull-out program, it is best to focus on the overarching standards.

> **BOX 3.2: COMMON CORE STANDARDS COLLEGE AND CAREER READINESS STANDARDS**
>
> W.7: Conduct short as well as more sustained research projects based on focused questions, demonstrating understanding of the subject under investigation.
>
> W.8: Gather relevant information from multiple print and digital sources, assess the credibility and accuracy of each source, and integrate the information while avoiding plagiarism.
>
> W.9: Draw evidence from literary or informational texts to support analysis, reflection, and research.
>
> R.10: Read and comprehend complex literary and informational texts independently and proficiently.
>
> (National Governors Association Center for Best Practices & Council of Chief State School Officers)

Tips for Lesson Design

The lessons and resources outlined in this book are suggested for educators who want to begin or continue the work of discussing social justice with gifted learners. They are meant to be adapted and modified for the needs of your students. As you continue reading, you'll see that building relationships is the number one priority when talking about social justice with your students. It is important to cultivate empathy and develop an activist mindset in your students before beginning these discussions.

This is not meant to be a prescribed curriculum. *Empowered Leaders* serves as a collection of resources that you can pick and choose to match the needs and identities of your students. We have provided it in a full unit format for consistency, but feel free to pull apart the pieces to create a curriculum that best suits your program and students' needs. We want educators to have the tools to facilitate equitable conversations and challenging projects about social justice.

Mentor text recommendations are provided in each chapter that are aligned to the standards and grade level themes. These recommendations range from picture books to poems to young adult chapter books. The list was created to represent a variety of narratives, diverse characters, and BIPOC authors.

Rubrics, project descriptions, mini-lessons and more are available to all educators throughout this book. This curriculum is geared towards gifted learners, but many aspects of it can be beneficial to all students.

Strategies to expand and introduce *Empowered Leaders*

Let's Talk About It

Centering student voice in the classroom is essential to talking about social justice. *Let's Talk About It* is an after-school program we run in our district. It is based on the Learning for Justice's (2020) guide called *Let's Talk* (https://www.learningforjustice.org/sites/default/files/2021-01/TT-Let-s-Talk-Publication-January-2020.pdf). Students drive the learning based on topics they are interested in.

You can use this framework in any learning environment. You can take the core ideas behind *Let's Talk About It* and infuse them in your classroom, small groups, or after-school program. The basic idea behind this group is student voice. Begin this process by allowing students to elect to stay afterschool for this program. Each week have the students choose a topic. In the beginning rounds of this group, it is okay for you, as the teacher, to run these sessions. As students become more comfortable with the format, allow them to facilitate all sessions. When you pick a new topic for the week, also pick a facilitator to prepare readings, visuals, and discussion questions. The more student voice present in this group, the more successful it will be. It is difficult at first for teachers to give up control and sit back and listen, but it is so important for the students to know that you are there to listen to them, not to control their ideas or discussions. As you build this kind of relationship with students, you will recognize that they have so much passion for these topics. You can begin incorporating what you learn from your students into your classroom as well.

The following are some tips for uplifting student voice in your classroom like we do in *Let's Talk About It*.

- Educators, listen more and talk less
- Share pronouns, if they feel comfortable doing so
- Collectively develop norms
- Define terms
- Encourage personal stories and reflection
- Ask open-ended questions
- Provide facts and research
- Let students drive the conversation

This framework for teaching social justice can easily be applied to the Schoolwide Enrichment Model. You can have sessions like *Let's Talk About It* during your lessons. This open-ended forum for students is similar to our next strategy – facilitating circles.

Circles

One of the best and most effective ways to build connections in the classroom and provoke discussion is by using circles. Based on Native American parliamentary techniques, this teaching strategy has been used to provide students with a safe and respectful space to express their opinions on topics (Jennings et al., 2015; Wolf & Rickard, 2003).

To start, let us look at it mathematically. The radius of a circle is the point from the center to the edge. In theory, all the radii in a single circle are equal. Translating that to the classroom, all the students are set equidistant from the center of the circle, giving them all equal footing in the space. This, along with other efforts outlined later, allows all students to feel like they are equally represented in the discussion.

First, let's look at how to start class off with a circle. Once your students are sitting or standing in a circle, you can proactively use it to get to know the individuals in front of you. Grab a stuffed animal or stress ball to use as a talking piece and pass it around the circle in order, asking the students a single, simple question. For example, you could ask them about their favorite color. Or ask them about what they do on the weekends. As time goes by and they get more comfortable with each other and with you, you can ask them what makes them sad, or what makes them angry. By coming together and being vulnerable, students will feel more like a family and be more responsive to targeted discussions on tense social issues. Remember, it is extremely important that you take part in these circles as well, to show that you're one with them.

One thing we have learned through the continual use of circles is that it is easier to just leave your desk in a circle for the entire year, not only to continue to build that community, but also it makes it easier to do these opening and closing circles before students break off into their groups to work. Another way would be to identify an area that your students can stand or sit in that isn't at their desks. This could be in the hallway right outside your room, on the carpet in the front, or even just around a pod of desks. By not having to move desks, you are minimizing transition time and maximizing instructional time (and you can use that language right on your post-observation reflection!).

For more in-depth guidelines and strategies for using basic proactive circles, the International Institute for Restorative Practices (IIRP) provides a lot of information on their website (https://www.iirp.edu) and through in-person trainings.

Another type of circle you can use is a Socratic seminar. This type of discussion follows the same general principles and theory as the proactive circles, but without the talking piece. In this scenario, students can talk at will. This type of circle focuses more on active thinking of open-ended ideas and moral dilemmas, rather than just questions with a single-word, or short-phrase answer like before. When we discuss social issues, we want the students' voices to be heard, not ours. If we do the talking, then we delve into corrupt territory, and open ourselves to pushing our ideological beliefs onto children. Socratic seminars allow for the exact opposite: by posing a question, and letting the students debate it with the teacher simply as a facilitator of conversation, students are the agents of discourse and change (Tredway, 1995).

Holding students accountable during discussions is extremely important as well and there are multiple ways to go about doing so. The first way is to have a piece of paper with all of the students' names written on it in a circle. Then when one student talks to another, draw an arrow between those two names on your paper. This is a very teacher-centric way of doing it, but often the easiest. Another way is to have the students track who has spoken. Students can use tally marks on a sticky note to denote when they speak, or for a more community-based method, they can identify a partner in the circle and tally any time that partner speaks. The accountability, though not the main point of the circle, is especially helpful during administrative observations, participation goals, and even future planning and grouping.

Social Contracts, Class Charters, & Community Ethos

Social contracts, class charters, and community agreements or ethos are all great ways for student voice to be heard when making the rules for the class, specifically around class discussions. We want students to feel heard and respected when they speak and allowing them to come up with this rule makes it even more meaningful. To create a social contract, have students brainstorm expectations for the classroom individually. We recommend listing the general categories or areas you want students to focus on. For example, in our classrooms, we use "During Work Time", "During Discussions", and "Always" as our three categories. In addition, you can add parts about how members of the class (students, teachers, guests, etc.) should be treated and repercussions for breaching the social contract. No matter what categories or formatting you use, make sure you take time to reflect on how to have a discussion and talk about issues that can be deemed "controversial". Next, have students share their ideas. Write them down on the board and discuss each one with the whole class. Finally, come up with a final, permanent list of norms on a piece of chart paper. Students should then come up and sign the contract, agreeing to follow all the norms posted. We recommend letting it rest for a day, revisiting it once more for final agreement before signing. This way, it allows students to think about what they are signing and not feel pressured to agree with it right away. Many of our contracts have been altered, with group consensus of course, between our original draft and our final copy.

Now that you have a social contract in place, you can refer to it before each of your circles or class discussions to make sure that students remember what the expectations are. With continued usage, students will start to hold each other accountable when it comes to the rules.

Blogs & Journals

Sometimes students are more comfortable starting in a place of privacy when grappling with social issues and journals are the perfect place for that. We like to implement blogging as a way for students to express themselves creatively as well as ideologically. Our students create and design Google Sites to journal their experiences throughout the year. Once or twice a month, we post questions for students to answer about the grade level themes or about their reactions to in-class discussions. For identity, we ask them about why it is important to call someone by their correct pronouns. For empathy, we ask them about scenarios and stories and have them write not only how they would react, but also how the prompt made them feel. Here, not only can we work on student writing, a goal of the Common Core Standards, but also make sure even our shyest of students get their voices heard.

These blogs also have a second and unintended use. They allow for the uniqueness of our students to come out. Students can, in their spare time, create other tabs and pages showing off favorite recipes, reviews of books and movies, their artistic endeavors, or even videos of their gymnastics competitions. Though it is not a graded part of the curriculum, it is often one of the students' favorite parts.

Choice Boards & Menus

Identity and empathy are huge topics. There is no possible way to cover it all, and nor should you! With social justice education and gifted education, it is best to provide students with multiple avenues to explore a facet that interests them. Choice boards and menus provide students with choice in their learning. There are many ways to do both boards and menus, and each have their pros and cons. First, menus provide students with groups of options to pick from. Think of when you go to a restaurant with a pre-fix menu; you pick one appetizer, one entrée, and one dessert. If you want to get creative, you can add other sections like side dishes and drinks as well. In each of these sections, select a group of activities that all related to each other. One year, we decided to change our 6th grade diversity choice board into a choice menu. The first section of the menu included three activities focused solely on what anti-racism is. We felt that it was important for students to be exposed to this theory so by changing to a menu, we ended up requiring all students to engage with anti-racism, while still maintaining a certain level of choice. The rest of the choice board squares were folded into the entrée and dessert parts of the menu, still requiring students to complete three activities. Menus provide more structure to your choices, allowing you to group them by theme or topic, but in doing so, limit choice.

Choice Boards, on the other hand, can range from simple to complex. For lower grades, it might be appropriate to only have three or four activities in a board, with students picking only one. A friend of ours who teaches science at the high school level has her students work through a 6x5, 30 square choice board, where each activity has a different point value. The goal in this one is to obtain a certain number of points, not engage with a certain number of squares. You can also do it so that the students have to pick three options in a row, like a tic-tac-toe board. In this text, we use a standard 3x3 choice board for each of the grade levels. A blank sample template is available in Appendix B and online in the digital resources.

No matter which version you do, we recommend always having a written portion associated with it so that you're holding students accountable for their learning. We've included a standard two activity and standard three activity response worksheet in Appendix F and Appendix G, as well as online.

Now it is time to delve into the curriculum we've created for our students and for you. Look out for these strategies and think about how you can best serve your students when teaching *Empowered Leaders*.

References

Ford, D. Y. (2011). *Multicultural gifted education*. (2nd ed.) Prufrock Press.

Jennings, L., Gandarilla, M., & Tan, P. P. (2015). Using the Native American Talking Circle: Experiential learning on ethnic and cultural diversity of Southern California. *Groupwork*, 25(1), 58–77.

Kleinrock, L. (2021). *Start here, start now: A guide to antibias and antiracist work in your school community*. Heinemann.

Learning for Justice. (2020) *Let's Talk: A Guide to Facilitating Critical Conversations with Students*. The Southern Poverty Law Center, 2019.

National Governors Association Center for Best Practices & Council of Chief State School Officers. (2010). *Common Core State Standards for English language arts and literacy in history/social studies, science, and technical subjects*. Authors.

Professional Standards Committee. (2019). *2019 Pre-K–Grade 12 Gifted Programming Standards*. National Association for Gifted Children.

Reis, S. M., & Peters, P. M. (2020). Research on the Schoolwide Enrichment Model: Four decades of insight, innovation, and evolution. *Gifted Education International*. doi:10.1177/0261429420963987

Reynolds, J., & Kendi, I. X. (2020). *Stamped: Anti-racism, racism, and you*. Little, Brown and Company.
Scott, M. T. (2014). Using the Blooms–Banks matrix to develop Multicultural Differentiated lessons for gifted students. *Gifted Child Today, 37*(3), 163–168. doi:10.1177/1076217514532275
Tredway, L. (1995). Socratic seminars: Engaging students in intellectual discourse. *Educational Leadership, 53*(1), 26–29.
Wolf, P. R., & Rickard, J. A. (2003). Talking Circles: A Native American Approach to Experiential Learning. *Journal of Multicultural Counseling and Development, 31*(1), 39–43. doi:10.1002/j.2161-1912.2003.tb00529.x

Chapter 4

Identity

Introduction to Identity

Who are you? That is the question that even we, as adults, ask ourselves. Normally for fourth graders, the answer isn't the biggest of deals. They still have a lot of growing to do! But when working with social justice topics like empathy, diversity, justice, and action, it is important to know where we all fit into society. Students need to understand that, whether they like it or not, society focuses on certain identities, dubbed social identity factors (Jewell, 2020). And these factors play a role in how people view them and potentially how they view themselves. But that is not the limit; there are factors that are important to fourth graders that should be embraced and celebrated. We have a student who loves praying mantises and wants to do every project on them. Another student is an amazing cartoonist who, anytime he has free time, continues one of the many comic strips in his notebook. Fourth grade is the perfect time for students to start embracing their personal identities and learning about all of the things that make them who they are.

This grade level also works to lay the groundwork for all the future grade level work to come. We find identity so important that even in eighth grade, before we begin the grade level theme of action, we spend the first few weeks of school reviewing identity and seeing how things have changed.

Learning for Justice Definition

What is identity?

- The collective aspect of the set of characteristics by which a thing or person is definitively recognized or known.
- The set of behavioral or personal characteristics by which an individual is recognizable as a member of a group.

(Learning for Justice, 2019)

DOI: 10.4324/9781003270539-4

> **BOX 4.1 LEARNING FOR JUSTICE ANCHOR STANDARDS**
>
> Learning for Justice's Social Justice Standards establishes the following five standards within the Identity domain.
>
> Students will:
>
> ID.1. develop positive social identities based on their membership in multiple groups in society;
> ID.2. develop language and historical and cultural knowledge that affirm and accurately describe their membership in multiple identity groups;
> ID.3. recognize that people's multiple identities interact and create unique and complex individuals;
> ID.4. express pride, confidence and healthy self-esteem without denying the value and dignity of other people; and
> ID.5. recognize traits of the dominant culture, their home culture and other cultures and understand how they negotiate their own identity in multiple spaces
>
> (Learning for Justice, 2019)

Essential Questions

- What is identity?
- How is identity developed?
- How does identity affect our relationships?

Unit Plan

This unit is structured as a ten-lesson unit plan. All the resources can be adapted to meet the needs of your students. Feel free to adapt the lesson to fit the needs of your program. At the top of each lesson is a general time frame that the lesson can be performed in. Oftentimes, we stretch our lesson plans over multiple days. We want you to use these lesson plans in whatever way best fits your programming.

Table 4.1 Grade 4 Identity Unit Overview

Week	Lessons	Learning Target
1	1–2	I can define identity.
2	3–4	I can explore how identity develops and affects our relationships.
3	5–6	I will draw conclusions from prior knowledge to identify and research a topic based on the theme of identity.
4	7–8	I will synthesize my research information into a complete product.
5	9–10	I will present my project to the class. I will provide TAG feedback on my peers' projects.

GRADE 4 IDENTITY

Lesson 1
Time: 45 Minutes

This lesson serves to assess your students' current understanding of identity so you can adapt your instruction moving forward.

Objective

Students will be able to demonstrate their understanding of how identity develops and affects our relationships.

Guiding Questions

How does identity develop?
How does identity affect our relationships?

Materials

- Theme Project Assessment
- Writing Rubric (see Appendix C)

Learning Activities

Write the word "IDENTITY" on the board. Have students take 5–10 minutes to write down what identity means to them using a brainstorming strategy of your choice. Possible examples include mind maps, brain dumps, graphic organizers, and KWL charts. Instruct them to include not only a definition, if they know one, but also factors that influence identity, as well as anything that reminds them of that word. The goal is to activate prior knowledge before starting the pre-test.

Next, instruct students to complete the Theme Project Assessment. This pre-assessment is a standard written response to the essential question of the unit. Each student will receive an individual copy of the assignment, either physically or through an online educational platform like Google Classroom. They can only use their brainstorm sheet for assistance.

Students most likely will not do well on this, but always remind them to try their best. At the end of the unit, they will most likely do a lot better.

Closure/Assessment

At the end of the lesson, have a student re-read the learning objective. Using a thumbs up/thumbs down system, ask students if they completed the objective to the best of their ability. Have two–three students share why they indicated yes or no.

Scaffold/Language/Extension

Since this is a pre-assessment, all students need to see a similar assessment. Please adjust as necessary based on special education and language goals.

36 Identity

Figure 4.1

Name: _____ Date: _____

Theme Project Assessment

Directions: Please answer the following questions in complete sentences. Use specific examples.

How does *identity* develop?

How does our *identity* affect our relationships?

_____
_____
_____
_____
_____
_____
_____
_____

**Grade 4
Identity**

Empowered Leaders: A Social Justice Curriculum for Gifted Learners

GRADE 4 IDENTITY

Lesson 2
Time: 45–90 Minutes

This lesson serves to introduce students to the grade level theme: identity.

Objectives

Students will be able to define identity.

Guiding Question

What is identity?

Materials

- Theme Project Workbook (Available Online)
- Paper and Writing Utensils

Learning Activities

Read the essential question (see Lesson 1) and brainstorm definitions as a class. Ask students to use the word in a sentence, provide examples from their life, and write down any questions they have.

BOX 4.2: DEFINITION OF IDENTITY

The collective aspect of the set of characteristics by which a thing or person is definitively recognized or known; the set of behavioral or personal characteristics by which an individual is recognizable as a member of a group.

(Learning for Justice, 2019)

Discuss the definition of identity as a whole group. Using the Theme Project Workbook, discuss in small groups what students know about identity. Then have students share out, creating a class model. Make sure students hit on a variety of identity markers that may be important to include such as race, gender, ability, family structure, etc.

Next, have students design their own identity map. They can use an online platform like Google Slides or Google Docs or they can use a piece of paper.

Closure/Assessment

At the end of the lesson, have a student re-read the learning objective. Ask if anyone can explain identity in their words. Also, allow time for students to volunteer to share aspects of their identity map with their peers.

Scaffold/Language/Extension

- Provide a graphic organizer similar to the one in the theme book for the students' personal identity maps.
- Use visuals and provide examples of identity markers.
- Do a pair and share instead of whole group when brainstorming the definition.
- Provide translations and allow students to write in their native languages.

GRADE 4 IDENTITY

Lesson 3
Time: 90–120 Minutes

This lesson serves to allow students to see examples of different identities.

Objectives

Students will be able to recognize different identity markers in literary and non-fiction examples.

Guiding Question

What are examples of different identity markers in fiction and in non-fiction writing?

Materials

- A diverse group of mentor texts (see list on p. 61)
- Identity Mentor Text Analysis Worksheet
- A short story related to identity
- Sticky Notes

Learning Activities

Have students brainstorm different identity markers on sticky notes. They can refer to their own identity maps for guidance. Write the word "IDENTITY" on the board and have students place their sticky notes around it.

Read a short text about identity. *My Shadow is Pink* by Scott Stuart and *Julian is a Mermaid* by Jessica Love are both great examples. As you read this example with your class, point out the identity factors of the characters.

Introduce the mentor texts available to them. We recommend identifying mentor texts based on student ability and/or interest. These should be books that are digestible in one sitting. These books will act as Type I experiences, getting students interested in one of the many facets of identity. The books should represent a variety of identities. See our mentor text list at the end of the chapter for reference.

Group students and assign them a mentor text. Also, provide students with the mentor text worksheet to help students keep track of information. You can check-in and conference with each of the groups throughout class.

If students are stuck, ask some of the following questions:

- What evidence from the text shows you this about the character's identity?
- What new identity markers did you learn about?
- How does the author develop the character's identity?

Closure/Assessment

Have each group share some of the things they learned about identity while reading the mentor texts.

Scaffold/Language/Extension

- Pre-assign groups by ability, interest, or behavior.
- Allow students to self-select into groups.
- Native-language copies of the mentor texts.
- Substitute the picture books for videos (ex. *Hair Love* by Matthew A. Cherry is based on the Oscar-winning short film of the same name) or audiobooks (Kendrick Sampson reads *Anti-Racist Baby* on Netflix Jr.'s YouTube Account) or provide these resources in addition to the physical book.

Figure 4.2

Name: _____ Date: _____

Identity Mentor Text Analysis

Directions: Take notes on each mentor text to answer the following questions. Make sure to cite specific page numbers. Be prepared to discuss your findings.

Title of Book	
Author	
Choose one character. What is their name?	
Circle the identity markers you know about that character.	Race Gender Family Structure Age Religion Ability Ethnicity Socio-Economic Status Education
Describe the character's identity from the book.	

Empowered Leaders: A Social Justice Curriculum for Gifted Learners

GRADE 4 IDENTITY

Lesson 4
Time: 45–90 Minutes

This lesson serves to allow students to investigate the aspects of identity that interest them.

Objective

Students will be able to explore identity through activities that interest them.

Guiding Questions

What are some examples of people's identities being celebrated? What are some examples of people being oppressed based on their identity?

Materials

- Identity Choice Board
- Choice Board Response Worksheet (see Appendix G)
- Sticky Notes and Chart Paper (Optional)

Learning Activities

Discuss the guiding questions with the students. Depending on prior knowledge, you may need to define what oppression means with your students. Have them share their initial thoughts on the guided question via a Jamboard or sticky notes and chart paper.

Then briefly introduce the choices available to them on the choice board. For more information on making choice boards, see Chapter 3. This lesson acts as another Type I experience for them, allowing them to experience different activities related to identity.

After students investigate two activities of the choice board or menu, ask students to write down their reactions using the Choice Board Worksheet and the embedded sentence starters.

Closure/Assessment

As a class, have at least two students share an example of identity and their reaction to it.

Scaffold/Language/Extension

- Allow early finishers to engage with other squares without having to write another reaction paragraph.
- Allow early finishers to start researching more about one of the squares.
- Provide students with a translated version of the article or subtitles for videos.
- Allow students to write in their native language.
- Allow students to work with a partner to discuss the articles after engaging with them independently. They should still write the reactions alone.

44　Identity

Figure 4.3

Name: _____ Date: _____

Choice Board

Directions: Choose two activities to complete. Write one paragraph detailing what you learned from these activities.

1. Read	2. Discuss	3. Research & Create
One book from your classroom and fill in the "Reading Diversity Checklist" from *Learning for Justice*	Different identity markers in your life with a partner or group	A cartoon, infographic, or word cloud about identity.
4. Interview	**5. Read**	**6. Read**
A friend who has a different identity marker from you	"Where's The Color In Kids' Lit? Ask The Girl With 1,000 Books (And Counting)" NPR	A picture book that features a main character who has a different identity than yours
7. Write	**8. Draw**	**9. Explore**
A paragraph describing the best part of you	A picture of someone that interests you	The Smithsonian Natural History Museum African Voices Exhibit

_____

_____

_____

_____ Grade **4**
_____ **Identity**

Empowered Leaders: A Social Justice Curriculum for Gifted Learners

GRADE 4 IDENTITY

Lesson 5
Time: 90 Minutes

This lesson serves to facilitate student choice in picking a topic that interests them.

Objective

Based on their personal interests, students will decide on a topic for their theme project.

Guiding Question

What interests you in relation to the grade level theme?

Materials

- Sticky Notes
- Theme Project Workbook (Available Online)

Learning Activities

Inform students that they are going to start researching a specific topic related to identity and that today's goal is to pick one of the topics from the list or come up with a new one.

Introduce the Theme Project workbook and provide each student with either a physical or digital copy to complete as they work through their project. They should not start on this until you approve their topic.

As a group, discuss potential topics related to identity. Ask students to think of things they've engaged with on the choice boards and with the mentor texts. Students can also use prior knowledge to come up with topics. Write them on the board or a piece of chart paper. This will be an anchor chart with additional topics for students to choose from.

Then students should start to think about potential topics related to their interests. Conference with students throughout the class to help narrow the students' thinking and provide new or additional options based on prior information gained from learning profiles and student interest.

Once students pick a topic, the student should start to work through the Theme Project Workbook.

Closure/Assessment

At the end of class, give each student a sticky note. Ask them to write their name and one topic that they think would make for a good theme project. If they cannot decide, remind them that this isn't a commitment, that they can still change it after class. You just want to see where their thoughts are at the moment. This section of sticky notes can also be used as a jumping off point for students in other classes who are not sure where to start in coming up with a topic.

Scaffold/Language/Extension

- Students can research in their native language.
- Students can research examples from their own cultures or others.
- Allow students to work in groups based on similar interests.
- Provide a list of approved topics.

Image 4.1

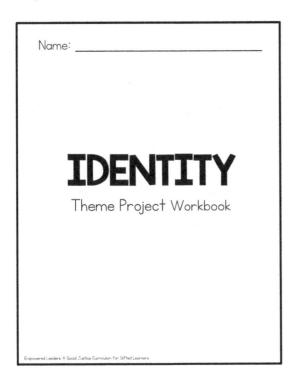

Name: ______________________

IDENTITY

Theme Project Workbook

Empowered Leaders: A Social Justice Curriculum for Gifted Learners

Image 4.2

Topic Brainstorm

Directions: List topics you are interested in related to the theme: identity.

Identity

Identity | Theme Project Workbook

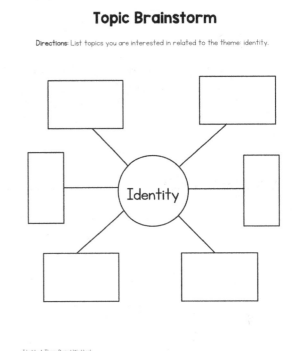

Image 4.3

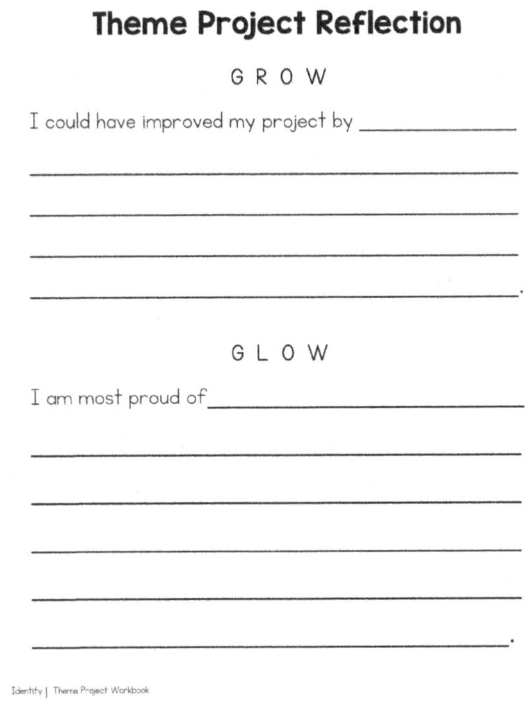

Theme Project Reflection

G R O W

I could have improved my project by ______________

____

____

____

______________________________.

G L O W

I am most proud of______________________

____

____

____

____

______________________________.

Identity | Theme Project Workbook

The Theme Project Workbook is available online under the digital resources page for this text.

GRADE 4 IDENTITY

Lesson 6
Time: 90 Minutes

This lesson serves to introduce students to researching and identifying credible sources.

Objective

Students will be able to locate sources on their topic
Students will be able to analyze their source for credibility.

Guiding Question

How do you know if a source is credible?

Materials

- CAPES Poster (available at https://www.brianhousand.com/uploads/2/4/2/8/2428164/fighting_fake_news_-_capes_poster_pdf.pdf)
- Theme Project Workbook (Available Online)

Learning Activities

Have students retrieve their sticky note from the wall. If they are planning to keep their initial topic, have them write a check mark and put the sticky note back on the wall. If they want to change their topic, ask them to cross out the topic they wrote and write the new one underneath.

Pick a topic of your own related to identity and model how you would find a reliable article on the internet. Also, show how to find a book from the library or an online database.

Once you showed your students *how* to find a research source, analyze that source using CAPES as a whole group. This strategy was created by Brian Housand and is featured in his text, *Fighting Fake News* (2018), available from Routledge. Annotate the article based on each section of CAPES. Have students answer the guiding questions along with you, based on the information in the model article.

- Credentials – Who is the author? What makes the author an expert? What is their bias?
- Accuracy – Is the information up to date? Is it based on facts? Where did the information come from?
- Purpose – What is the purpose? Inform? Entertain? Satire? Parody? Advertisement? News?
- Emotion – Is the site designed to evoke an emotional response? How does the site make you feel?
- Support – What supporting evidence can you find from another site?

Then, provide time for students to work independently on in groups. They need to pick one article from their research to analyze for CAPES. This lesson can be repeated as many times as you need while the students get comfortable researching and analyzing sources.

For another lesson on finding reliable sources, check out Learning for Justice's lesson here: https://www.learningforjustice.org/classroom-resources/lessons/evaluating-reliable-sources

Closure/Assessment

At the end of the lesson, ask students to identify one way to tell if a source is credible or not. Have two students share out loud.

Scaffold/Language/Extension

- Early finishers can analyze another source based on CAPES.
- Early finishers can start working on their product.
- Provide a list of reliable sources for students to start with.
- Students can find research articles in their native language.
- Students can use a graphic organizer with CAPES to guide their analysis.

GRADE 4 IDENTITY

Lesson 7
Time: 45–90 Minutes

This lesson serves to give students time to research. This lesson can and should be repeated until students have enough information to start creating their product.

Objective

Students will research information related to their Theme Project topic.

Guiding Question

How does all of the research come together to fit into a final product?

Materials

- Theme Project Workbook (Available Online)
- Sticky Notes

Learning Activities

Students will work on finishing the research pages of the Theme Project Workbook.
    While they are researching, conference with students about their research notes so far.
    Provide them with group or individual support in finding research related to their topic. This would also be a great time to visit your library media specialist for a mini lesson on finding a nonfiction book in the library.

Closure/Assessment

Have students write on a sticky note, one thing they realized about their topic when working on the research notes pages of their workbook. Ask two students to share.

Scaffold/Language/Extension

- Early finishers can dive deeper into the research.
- Early finishers can start working on their product.
- Some students may need help finding sources and coming up with a space on the whiteboard for students to write databases and website that were helpful to them might assist others.
- Students can focus on sources in their native language.
- Students can continue to work together, if allowed.

GRADE 4 IDENTITY

Lesson 8
Time: 45–90 Minutes

This lesson serves to introduce students to the various product types they can select for their Theme Project.

Objective

Students will identify the components of a quality final product.

Guiding Question

What are the components of a quality final product?

Materials

- Theme Project Workbook (Available Online)
- Project Materials (This is teacher- and student-based. We like to have a plethora of materials available to students from podcast microphones to construction paper and glue, to iPads. Make sure to introduce to your students the materials that you have available.)
- Past Theme Projects (if available)
- Theme Project Rubric (see Appendix D)
- Product List (see Appendix E)

Learning Activities

Ask students to look at the Theme Project Rubric. Have them circle components from the rubric that they feel are important for a quality product. Discuss as a whole group how a rubric works and how they will be graded.

Remind students that their product can be anything, a podcast, a short story, a painting, an exhibit, a diorama, a Jeopardy game, or even a poster. Through past experience, we like to limit the use of Google Slides or PowerPoint presentations. These usually tend to be very surface level. If a student is adamant about doing one, we suggest asking them to research what makes a good presentation, and then having them record their presentation for the feedback portion of the unit.

Students can then come up and look at the past examples, if available. Once they are done, they can get to work on their product. Walk around the room, conference with students, and provide assistance in getting materials and/or using software.

Closure/Assessment

Ask students to show, using zero to two fingers, how many more classes of project work time they need. Use this information to plan instruction going further.

Repeat the individual work time and conferencing portion of this lesson for as many classes as needed. Make sure students self-assess and edit their projects before turning them in.

Scaffold/Language/Extension

- Provide students with a modified workbook for IEP or 504 accommodations.
- Provide feedback to students, pushing them to dig further into their topic, adding more depth to their project.

GRADE 4 IDENTITY

Lesson 9
Time: 45–90 Minutes

This lesson allows students to get feedback on their projects from their peers.

Objective
Students will provide constructive TAG feedback to three peers' projects.

Guiding Question
What are some ways that I can improve my project for next year?

Materials

- Completed Theme Projects
- TAG Feedback Worksheet

Learning Activities

Briefly discuss TAG feedback with the students. TAG Feedback was created by Concourse Village Elementary School in Bronx, NY. It stands for Tell, Ask, Give and is a popular way for students to provide meaningful feedback to their peers. Provide students with copies of the TAG Feedback Sentence Starters.

Have each student set up their project at their desk with the TAG Feedback Sentence Starters and Peer Feedback Worksheets laid out in front. Instruct students that they will be providing feedback on two peers. They are to leave both TAG sheets on their desk and move around only with a writing utensil. Have the students move to a new station and provide TAG feedback. Set up a 10-minute timer. When the timer ends, they are to move to another desk and provide TAG feedback on the next person's project. Repeat this step twice.

Closure/Assessment

Have students review the feedback and make any necessary changes to the project. If they feel confident in their work, they can formally submit their projects. Otherwise, we suggest making the project due at the beginning of next class.

Ask students using a thumbs up/thumbs down, how helpful their peers' feedback was.

Scaffold/Language/Extension

- Students with language barriers can work together on providing feedback or use Google Translate to provide feedback to English-speaking peers.

Figure 4.4

T.A.G. Feedback

		Sentence Starters
T	Tell them something you liked	_____ stuck with me because... I really appreciated _____ because.... This is high quality work because... I really like _____ because...
A	Ask them a question	Can you further explain _____ because... What did you mean by... I don't understand... Why...
G	Give them a suggestion	One way to improve your project is... I wish you included... because... I would suggest... I think your project could be even better by...

- -

Project Author(s):

T	Tell them something you liked	
A	Ask them a question	
G	Give them a suggestion	

Your name:

Empowered Leaders: A Social Justice Curriculum for Gifted Learners

GRADE 4 IDENTITY

Lesson 10
Time: 45 Minutes

This lesson serves to assess students' current understanding of identity.

Objective

Students will be able to demonstrate their understanding of how identity develops and affects our relationships.

Guiding Question

How does identity develop?
How does identity affect our relationships?

Materials

- Theme Project Assessment
- Writing Rubric (see Appendix C)

Learning Activities

Write the word "IDENTITY" on the board. Have students take 5–10 minutes to write down what identity means to them using a brainstorming strategy of your choice. Possible examples include mind maps, brain dumps, graphic organizers, and KWL charts. Instruct them to include not only a definition, if they know one, but also factors that influence identity, as well as anything that reminds them of that word. The goal is to activate prior knowledge before starting the post-test.

Next, instruct students to complete the Theme Project Assessment. This post-assessment is a standard written response to the essential question of the unit. Each student will receive an individual copy of the assignment, either physically or through an online educational platform like Google Classroom. They can only use their brainstorm sheet for assistance.

Students should be able to demonstrate a better understanding of identity in this assessment compared to the beginning of the unit.

Then, as a whole class, reflect on the assessment, project, and unit.

Closure/Assessment

Using a sticky note, what is one way that this unit can be improved for next year?

Scaffold/Language/Extension

Since this is a post-assessment, all students need to see a similar assessment. Make adjustments necessary based on special education and language goals.

Figure 4.1

Name: _____ Date: _____

Theme Project Assessment

Directions: Please answer the following questions in complete sentences. Use specific examples.

How does *identity* develop?
How does our *identity* affect our relationships?

**Grade 4
Identity**

Empowered Leaders: A Social Justice Curriculum for Gifted Learners

Grade 4 Mentor Texts

We compiled this list of mentor texts to use as a supplement to any of the previous materials. The mentor texts are connected to identity, appropriate for gifted fourth grade students, and represent a range of narratives, writing styles, and authors. Most of the titles listed are picture books. If you are looking for more chapter books, check out the Grade 5 Mentor Texts in the next chapter. Additionally, many of the books can apply to multiple topics.

Figure 4.5

Identity Mentor Texts

Topic	Fiction Book Title & Authors	Non-Fiction Book Title & Authors
Class	*The Last Stop on Market Street* By Matt de la Peña *Those Shoes* By Maribeth Boelts *Maddi's Fridge* By Lois Brandt	*Poverty and Hunger* By Louise A. Spilsbury *Dear Librarian* By Lydia M. Sigwarth
Environment	*The Fog* By Kyo Maclear *The Lonely Polar Bear* By Khoa Le	*We are Water Protectors* By Carol Lindstrom *The Shark Lady* By Jess Keating
Gender	*Julian is a Mermaid* By Jessica Love	*It Feels Good to be Yourself* By Theresa Thorn
Immigration	*The Proudest Blue* By Ibtihaj Muhammad *Islandborn* By Junot Diaz	*Her Right Foot* By Dave Eggers *The Lost and Found Cat* By Doug Kuntz & Amy Shrodes
LGBTQ+	*George* by Alex Gino *When Aidan Became a Brother* By Kyle Lukoff and Kaylani Juanita	*Pride* By Rob Sanders *Stonewall* By Rob Sanders
Race	*Anti-Racist Baby* By Ibram X. Kendi	*A Kids Book About Racism* By Jelani Memory
Religion	*In My Mosque* By M. O. Yuksel	*The Brave Cyclist: The True Story of a Holocaust Hero* By Amalia Hoffman

Empowered Leaders: A Social Justice Curriculum for Gifted Learners

References

Housand, B. C. (2018). *Fighting fake news!: Teaching critical thinking and media literacy in a digital age*. Prufrock Press.

Jewell, T. (2020). *This book is anti-racist*. Frances Lincoln Children's Books.

Learning for Justice. (2019). *Learning for Justice Social Justice Anchor Standards*. The Southern Poverty Law Center.

Chapter 5

Empathy

Introduction to Empathy

Empathy is one of the most important concepts we can teach children. The earlier we can foster empathy in a child's development, the more likely they will grow up to become empowered and empathetic leaders.

We find that a great way to approach this theme is by incorporating multiple perspectives into your curriculum and teaching. This does not mean just during this unit, but during all other units moving forward. For students, texts can provide great insight into cultural, religious, and ethnic backgrounds different from their own. They can also provide true affirmation for the way they live their lives if their identity is reflected in a text. Teaching students how to respond to differences and how to empathize with other's stories will not only make your classroom a safer and more accepting place, but also the world at large.

Empathy is not a *Learning for Justice* Social Justice Standard on its own, but it is embedded throughout all the resources on its website. We believe that empathy stood out as an important topic for gifted children. Oftentimes, it is hard for gifted children to empathize with others, especially if they are isolated from their peers socially. With the tools to identify empathy through multiple perspectives in fictional stories, we found students began to see it in real world examples and their own lives as well.

Definition

What is empathy?

> The ability to share someone else's feelings or experiences by imagining what it would be like to be in that person's situation.
>
> (Cambridge University Press, 2021)

DOI: 10.4324/9781003270539-5

Essential Question

How do we foster empathy through multiple perspectives?

Unit Plan

This unit is structured as a ten-lesson unit plan. All the resources can be adapted to meet the needs of your students. Feel free to adapt the lesson to fit the needs of your program. At the top of each lesson is a general time frame that the lesson can be performed in. Oftentimes, we stretch our lesson plans over multiple days. We want you to use these lesson plans in whatever way best fits your programming.

Table 5.1 Grade 5 Empathy Unit Overview

Week	Lessons	Learning Target
1	1–2	I can define empathy.
2	3–4	I can recognize how to foster empathy through multiple perspectives.
3	5–6	I will draw conclusions from prior knowledge to identify and research a topic based on the theme of empathy.
4	7–8	I will synthesize my research information into a complete product.
5	9–10	I will present my project to the class. I will provide TAG feedback on my peers' projects.

GRADE 5 EMPATHY

Lesson 1
Time: 45 Minutes

This lesson serves to assess your students' current understanding of empathy so you can adapt your instruction moving forward.

Objective

Students will be able to demonstrate their understanding of how to foster empathy through the understanding of multiple perspectives.

Guiding Questions

How do we foster empathy through multiple perspectives?

Materials

- Theme Project Assessment
- Writing Rubric (see Appendix C)

Learning Activities

Write the word "EMPATHY" on the board. Have students take 5–10 minutes to write down what empathy means to them using a brainstorming strategy of your choice. Possible examples include mind maps, brain dumps, graphic organizers, and KWL charts. Instruct them to include not only a definition, but also anything that reminds them of that word. The goal is to activate prior knowledge before starting the pre-assessment.

Next, instruct students to complete an open-ended response to the essential question. This pre-assessment is a standard written response to the essential question of the unit. Each student will receive an individual copy of the assignment, either physically or through an online educational platform like Google Classroom. They can only use their brainstorm sheet for assistance.

Students most likely will not do well on this, but always remind them to try their best. At the end of the unit, they will most likely do a lot better.

Closure/Assessment

At the end of the lesson, have a student re-read the learning objective. Using a thumbs up/thumbs down system, ask students if they completed the objective to the best of their ability. Have two–three students share why they indicated yes or no.

Scaffold/Language/Extension

Since this is a pre-assessment, all students need to see a similar assessment. Please adjust as necessary based on special education and language goals.

Empathy 67

Figure 5.1

Name: _____ Date: _____

Theme Project Assessment

Directions: Please answer the following question in complete sentences. Use specific examples.

> How do we foster *empathy* through multiple perspectives?

_____
_____
_____
_____
_____
_____
_____
_____

**Grade 5
Empathy**

Empowered Leaders: A Social Justice Curriculum for Gifted Learners

GRADE 5 EMPATHY

Lesson 2
Time: 45–90 Minutes

This lesson serves to introduce students to the grade level theme: empathy.

Objective

Students will be able to define empathy.

Guiding Question

What is empathy?

Materials

- Chart Paper
- Markers

Learning Activities

Read the essential question (see Lesson 1) and brainstorm definitions as a class. Ask students to use the word in a sentence, provide examples from their life, and write down any questions they have.

Review the definition of identity if the students used this curriculum in the past.

BOX 5.1: DEFINITION OF IDENTITY

The collective aspect of the set of characteristics by which a thing or person is definitively recognized or known; the set of behavioral or personal characteristics by which an individual is recognizable as a member of a group.

(Learning for Justice, 2019)

> **BOX 5.2: DEFINITION OF EMPATHY**
>
> The ability to share someone else's feelings or experiences by imagining what it would be like to be in that person's situation.
>
> (Cambridge University Press, 2021)

Write each of the following questions on a separate piece of chart paper. Hang up 4 pieces of chart paper around the classroom.

1) What is empathy?
2) What does empathy look like to you?
3) Why is it important to learn about topics from multiple perspectives?
4) Draw a picture that represents empathy.

* For Hybrid or Remote Learning, use Padlet or Nearpod. Have each question be a new column, changing "Draw" to "Add" in the final question.

Have students rotate to each of the stations and write down answers for each question. There is no required format for answering the questions; blurbs, complete sentences, or drawings are all allowed. Once done, have students do one final walk through to review their peer's responses. Discuss as a group the trends they noticed.

Closure/Assessment

At the end of the lesson, have a student re-read the essential question. Give them each a sticky note or small piece of paper. Tell them to write a number, 1 through 5, on the back of the sticky note to indicate their understanding of empathy, 1 being "I don't understand it at all" to 5 being "I understand it completely and fully". On the front, have them write an "Ah-ha" moment or something they learned today.

Scaffold/Language/Extension

- Allow students to write on a piece of paper or sticky note instead of chart paper.
- Provide questions ahead of time in a worksheet format.
- Do a pair and share instead of a gallery walk, when using individual sheets.
- Provide translations of the questions and allow students to write in their native language.

GRADE 5 EMPATHY

Lesson 3
Time: 45–90 Minutes

This lesson serves to allow students to read stories with multiple perspectives.

Objectives

Students will be able to recognize multiple perspectives in literary and non-fiction examples.

Guiding Question

What are examples of multiple perspectives in fiction and in non-fiction writing?

Materials

- A diverse group of mentor texts (see list on p. 92)
- Empathy Mentor Text Analysis Worksheet
- A short story related to empathy

Learning Activities

Read a short text with an example of empathy present. *Thank You, M'am* by Langston Hughes is a great example. As you read this example with your class, point out the examples of empathy as well as talking about multiple perspectives.

After you model this, tell the students they will be analyzing one mentor texts of their own. This activity works great with picture books or chapter books. It also is helpful if they have already read the books. If they haven't, this lesson may be completed over a couple of days to incorporate reading time, depending on how lengthy the texts are.

Introduce the mentor texts available to them. We recommend identifying mentor texts based on student ability and/or interest. These books will act as a beginning Type I experiences, getting students interested in one of the many facets of empathy. The books should represent a variety of perspectives. See our mentor text list for reference.

Students can be grouped based on the mentor text or analyze it individually. Students can use the worksheet to guide their analysis. Check-in and conference with each of the groups throughout class.

Closure/Assessment

Have each group share some of the things they learned about empathy while reading the mentor texts.

Scaffold/Language/Extension

- Pre-assign groups by ability, interest, or behavior.
- Allow students to self-select into groups.
- Native-language copies of the mentor texts.
- Require students to analyze two mentor texts.
- Early finishers can look at multiple texts.

Empathy

Name: _____ Date: _____

Empathy Mentor Text Analysis

Directions: Take notes on each mentor text to answer the following questions. Make sure to cite specific page numbers. Be prepared to discuss your findings.

	Mentor Text #1
Title of Book	
Author	
Describe an example of empathy from the book.	
	Mentor Text #2
Title of Book	
Author	
Describe an example of empathy from the book.	
	Compare & Contrast
Compare and contrast the two examples of empathy.	

Empowered Leaders: A Social Justice Curriculum for Gifted Learners

Figure 5.2

GRADE 5 EMPATHY

Lesson 4
Time: 45–90 Minutes

This lesson serves to allow students to investigate the aspects of empathy that interest them.

Objective

Students will be able to explore empathy through activities that interest them.

Guiding Questions

What are some examples of empathy in the real world?

Materials

- Empathy Choice Board
- Choice Board Response Worksheet (see Appendix G)

Learning Activities

Have students think of one example of empathy in the real world. These can be examples from their lives (ex. Sharing toys with a sibling) or examples they've seen on the news (ex. the feel-good story at the end of a newscast). Ask three students to share out their examples. Like the previous lesson, this can also be used as a "Do Now" or "Bellringer"

Then briefly introduce the choices available to them on the Choice Board. For more information on making choice boards, see Chapter 3. This lesson acts as another Type I experience for them, allowing them to experience different activities related to diversity.

After students investigate two activities of the choice board or menu, ask students to write down their reactions using the Choice Board Worksheet and the embedded sentence starters.

Closure/Assessment

As a class, have at least three students share an example of empathy and their reaction to it.

Scaffold/Language/Extension

- Allow early finishers to engage with other squares without having to write another reaction paragraph.
- Allow early finishers to start researching more about one of the squares.
- Provide students with a translated version of the article or subtitles for videos.
- Allow students to write in their native language.
- Allow students to work with a partner to discuss the articles after engaging with them independently. They should still write the reactions alone.
- Allow students to find their own activities for the choice board. Consider including a free space!

Figure 5.3

Empathy 75

Name: _____ Date: _____

Choice Board

Directions: Choose two activities to complete. Write one paragraph detailing what you learned from these activities.

1. Read	2. Discuss	3. Research & Create
Thank you, Ma'am By Langston Hughes	Examples of empathy in your life with a partner or group	A cartoon, infographic, or word cloud about empathy.
4. Watch	**5. Read**	**6. Read**
Mix It Up at Lunch Day on Learning for Justice	*Those Shoes* By MaribEXeth Boelts	*Min Lee's Lunch* By Liz Kleinrock on Learning for Justice
7. Watch	**8. Explore**	**9. Read & Take Quiz**
Kid President's 20 Things We Should Say More Often	Stopbullying.gov	"The barrier-breaking power of learning someone else's story" on NewsELA

_____
_____
_____
_____

Grade **5**
Empathy

Empowered Leaders: A Social Justice Curriculum for Gifted Learners

GRADE 5 EMPATHY

Lesson 5
Time: 90 Minutes

This lesson serves to help students decide on a topic for their Theme Project.

Objective

Based on their personal interests, students will decide on a topic for their theme project.

Guiding Question

What interests you in relation to the grade level theme?

Materials

- Sticky Notes
- Theme Project Workbook (Available Online)

Learning Activities

Inform students that they are going to start researching a specific topic related to empathy. Introduce the Theme Project Workbook and provide each student with either a physical or digital copy to complete as they work through their project. They should not start on this until you approve their topic.

As a group, discuss potential topics related to empathy. Ask students to think of things they've engaged with on the choice boards and with the mentor texts. Students can also use prior knowledge to come up with topics. Write them on the board or a piece of chart paper. This will be an anchor chart with additional topics for students to choose from.

Then students should start to think about potential topics related to their interests. Conference with students throughout the class to help narrow the students' thinking and provide new or additional options based on prior information gained from learning profiles and student interest.

Once students pick a topic, the student should start to work through the Theme Project Workbook. They can complete the Topic Form page after you have approved their topic idea.

Closure/Assessment

At the end of class, give each student a sticky note. Ask them to write their name and one topic that they think would make for a good theme project. If they cannot decide, remind them that this isn't a commitment, that they can still change it after class. You just want to see where their thoughts are at the moment. This section of sticky notes can also be used as a jumping-off point for students in other classes who are not sure where to start in coming up with a topic.

Scaffold/Language/Extension

- Students can research in their native language.
- Students can research examples from their own cultures or others.
- Allow students to work in groups based on similar interests.
- Provide a list of approved topics.

Empathy

Image 5.1

Image 5.2

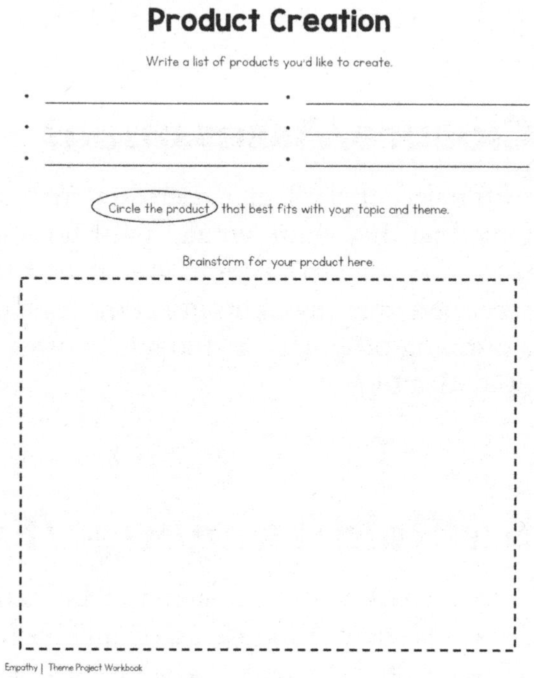

Image 5.3

The Theme Project Workbook is available online under the digital resources page for this text.

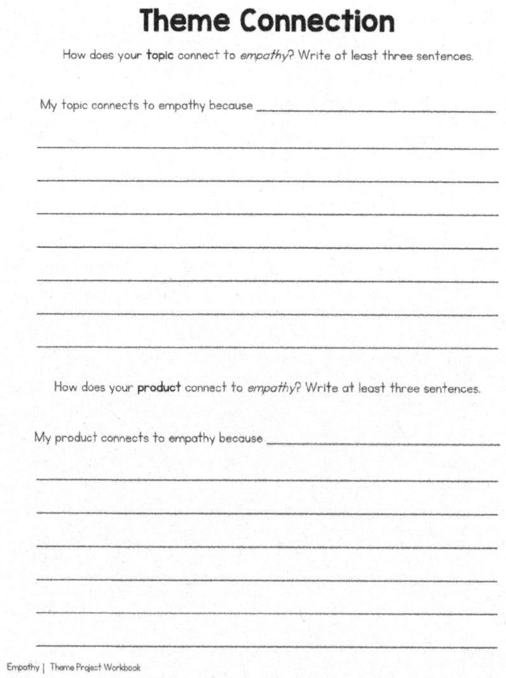

GRADE 5 EMPATHY

Lesson 6
Time: 45 Minutes

This lesson serves to introduce students to researching and identifying credible sources.

Objective

Students will be able to locate sources on their topic
Students will be able to analyze their source for credibility.

Guiding Question

How do you know if a source is credible?

Materials

- CAPES Poster (available at https://www.brianhousand.com/uploads/2/4/2/8/2428164/fighting_fake_news_-_capes_poster_pdf.pdf)
- Theme Project Workbook (Available Online)

Learning Activities

Have students retrieve their sticky note from the wall. If they are planning to keep their initial topic, have them write a check mark and put the stick note back on the wall. If they want to change their topic, ask them to cross out the topic they wrote and write the new one underneath.

Pick a topic of your own related to empathy and model how you would find a reliable article on the internet. Also, show how to find a book from the library or an online source.

Once you have shown your students *how* to find a research source, analyze that source using CAPES as a whole group. This strategy was created by Brian Housand and is featured in his text, *Fighting Fake News* (2018), available from Routledge. Annotate the article based on each section of CAPES. Have students answer the guiding questions along with you, based on the information in the model article.

- Credentials – Who is the author? What makes the author an expert? What is their bias?
- Accuracy – Is the information up to date? Is it based on facts? Where did the information come from?
- Purpose – What is the purpose? Inform? Entertain? Satire? Parody? Advertisement? News?
- Emotion – Is the site designed to evoke an emotional response? How does the site make you feel?
- Support – What supporting evidence can you find from another site?

Then, provide time for students to work independently on in groups. They need to pick one article to analyze for CAPES, based on their own topic. This lesson can be repeated as many times as you need while the students get comfortable researching and analyzing sources.

For another lesson on finding reliable sources, check out Learning for Justice's lesson here: https://www.learningforjustice.org/classroom-resources/lessons/evaluating-reliable-sources

Closure/Assessment

At the end of the lesson, ask students to identify one way to tell if a source is credible or not. Have two students share out loud.

Scaffold/Language/Extension

- Early finishers can analyze another source based on CAPES.
- Early finishers can start working on their product.
- Provide a list of reliable sources for students to start with.
- Students can find research articles in their native language.
- Students can use a graphic organizer with CAPES to guide their analysis.

GRADE 5 EMPATHY

Lesson 7
Time: 45–90 Minutes

This lesson serves to give students time to research. This lesson can and should be repeated until students have enough information to start creating their product.

Objective

Students will research information related to their Theme Project Topic.

Guiding Question

How does all of the research come together to fit into a final product?

Materials

- Theme Project Workbook (Available Online)
- Sticky Notes

Learning Activities

Students will work on finishing the research pages of the Theme Project Workbook.
    While they are researching, conference with students about their research notes so far.
    Provide them with group or individual support in finding research related to their topic. This would also be a great time to visit your library media specialist for a mini lesson in databases.

Closure/Assessment

Have students write on a sticky note, one thing they realized about their topic when working on the research notes pages of their workbook. Ask two students to share.

Scaffold/Language/Extension

- Early finishers can dive deeper into the research.
- Early finishers can start working on their product.
- Provide a list of reliable websites and databases.
- Students can find sources in their native language.
- Students can work together.

GRADE 5 EMPATHY

Lesson 8
Time: 45–90 Minutes

This lesson serves to introduce students to the various product types they can select for their Theme Project.

Objective

Students will identify the components of a quality final product.

Guiding Question

What are the components of a quality final product?

Materials

- Theme Project Workbook (Available Online)
- Project Materials (This is teacher- and student-based. We like to have a plethora of materials available to students from podcast microphones to construction paper and glue, to iPads. Make sure to introduce to your students the materials that you have available.)
- Past Theme Projects (if available)
- Theme Project Rubric (see Appendix D)
- Product List (see Appendix E)

Learning Activities

Ask students to look at the Theme Project Rubric. Have them circle components from the rubric that they feel are important for a quality product. Discuss as a whole group how a rubric works and how they will be graded.

Remind students that their product can be anything, a podcast, a short story, a painting, an exhibit, a diorama, a Jeopardy game, or even a poster. Through past experience, we like to limit the use of Google Slides or PowerPoint presentations. These usually tend to be very surface level. If a student is adamant about doing one, we suggest asking them to research what makes a good presentation, and then having them record their presentation for the feedback portion of the unit.

Students can then come up and look at the past examples, if available. Once they are done, they can get to work on their product. Walk around the room, conference with students, and provide assistance in getting materials and/or using software.

Closure/Assessment

Ask students to show, using zero to two fingers, how many more classes of project work time they need. Use this information to plan instruction going further.

Repeat the individual work time and conferencing portion of this lesson for as many classes as needed. Make sure students self-assess and edit their projects before turning it in.

Scaffold/Language/Extension

- Provide students with a modified workbook for IEP or 504 accommodations.
- Provide feedback to students, pushing them to dig further into their topic, adding more depth to their project.

GRADE 5 EMPATHY

Lesson 9
Time: 45–90 Minutes

This lesson allows students to get feedback on their projects from their peers.

Objective

Students will provide constructive TAG feedback to two peers' projects.

Guiding Question

What are some ways that I can improve my project for next year?

Materials

- Theme Projects
- TAG Feedback Worksheet

Learning Activities

Briefly discuss TAG feedback with the students. TAG Feedback was created by Concourse Village Elementary School in Bronx, NY. TAG stands for Tell, Ask, Give and is a popular way for students to provide meaningful feedback to their peers. Provide students with the TAG Feedback worksheet, which includes sentence starters.

Have each student set up their project at their desk with the TAG Feedback Sentence Starters and Peer Feedback Worksheets laid out in front. Instruct students that they will be providing feedback on two peers. They are to leave both TAG sheets on their desk and move around only with a writing utensil. Have the students move to a new station and provide TAG feedback. Set up a 10-minute timer. When the timer ends, they are to move to another desk and provide TAG feedback on the next person's project. Repeat this step twice.

Closure/Assessment

Have students review the feedback and make any necessary changes to the project. If they feel confident in their work, they can formally submit their projects. Otherwise, we suggest making the project due at the beginning of next class.

Ask students, using a thumbs up/thumbs down, how helpful their peers' feedback was.

Scaffold/Language/Extension

- Students with language barriers can work together on providing feedback or use Google Translate to provide feedback to English speaking peers.
- Students can complete TAG Feedback in pairs or small groups.

Figure 5.4

T.A.G. Feedback

		Sentence Starters
T	Tell them something you liked	_____ stuck with me because... I really appreciated _____ because.... This is high quality work because... I really like _____ because...
A	Ask them a question	Can you further explain _____ because... What did you mean by... I don't understand... Why...
G	Give them a suggestion	One way to improve your project is... I wish you included... because... I would suggest... I think your project could be even better by...

- -

Project Author(s):		
T	Tell them something you liked	
A	Ask them a question	
G	Give them a suggestion	
Your name:		

Empowered Leaders: A Social Justice Curriculum for Gifted Learners

GRADE 5 EMPATHY

Lesson 10
Time: 45 Minutes

This lesson serves as a post-assessment for the Theme Project Unit.

Objective

Students will be able to demonstrate their understanding of how understanding multiple perspectives can foster empathy

Guiding Question

How can understanding multiple perspectives foster empathy?

Materials

- Theme Project Assessment
- Writing Rubric (see Appendix C)
- Sticky Notes

Learning Activities

Write the word "EMPATHY" on the board. Have students take 5–10 minutes to write down what empathy means to them using a brainstorming strategy of your choice. Possible examples include mind maps, brain dumps, graphic organizers, and KWL charts. Instruct them to include not only a definition, if they know one, but also anything that reminds them of that word. The goal is to activate prior knowledge before starting the post-test.

Next, instruct students to complete the Theme Project Assessment. This post-assessment is a standard written response to the essential question of the unit. Each student will receive an individual copy of the assignment, either physically or through an online educational platform like Google Classroom. They can only use their brainstorm sheet for assistance.

Students should be able to demonstrate a better understanding of empathy in this assessment compared to the beginning of the unit.

Then, as a whole class, reflect on the assessment, project, and unit.

Closure/Assessment

Using a sticky note, what is one way that this unit can be improved for next year?

Scaffold/Language/Extension

Since this is a post-assessment, all students need to see a similar assessment. Make adjustments necessary based on special education and language goals.

Empathy

Figure 5.1

Name: _____ Date: _____

Theme Project Assessment

Directions: Please answer the following question in complete sentences. Use specific examples.

How do we foster *empathy* through multiple perspectives?

_____
_____
_____
_____
_____
_____
_____
_____

Grade 5
Empathy

Empathy Mentor Texts

We compiled this list of mentor texts to use as a supplement to any of the previous materials. The mentor texts are connected to empathy, appropriate for gifted fifth grade students, and represent a range of narratives, writing styles, and authors. Most of the titles listed are chapter books. If you are looking for more picture books, check out the Grade 4 Mentor Texts in the previous chapter. Additionally, many of the books can apply to multiple topics.

Empathy

Figure 5.5

Empathy Mentor Texts

Topic	Fiction Book Title & Authors	Non-Fiction Book Title & Authors
Class	*How to Steal a Dog* By Barbara O'Connor *A Wish in the Dark* By Christina Soontornvat	*Where Children Sleep* By James Mollison
Environment	*The Wild Robot* By Peter Brown *Hello Universe* By Erin Entrada	*The Boy Who Harnessed the Wind* By William Kamkwamba *Earth Heroes* By Lily Dyu
Gender	*The Moon Within* By Aida Salazar	*Pink, Blue and You!: Questions for Kids about Gender Stereotypes* By Elise Gravel
Immigration	*Dancing Home* By Alma Flor Ada and Gabriel M. Zubizarreta *I Lived on Butterfly Hill* By Marjorie Agosin	*A Kids Book About Immigration* By MJ Calderon *This Land is Our Land: A History of American Immigration* By Linda Barret Osborne
LGBTQ+	*Gracefully Grayson* By Amy Polonsky *Lily and Dunkin* By Donna Gephart	*Be Amazing: A History of Pride* By Desmond is Amazing
Race	*Blended* By Sharon M. Draper *What Lane?* By Torrey Maldanado	*Stamped (For Kids)* By Jason Reynolds & Ibram X. Kendi *Black Boy Joy* Edited By Kwame Mbalia
Religion	*Amina's Voice* By Hena Khan & Soneela Nankani	*We Had to Be Brave* By Deborah Hopkinson

Empowered Leaders: A Social Justice Curriculum for Gifted Learners

References

Cambridge University Press. (2021). Empathy. In *Cambridge Advanced Learner's Dictionary & Thesaurus*. https://dictionary.cambridge.org/us/dictionary/english/empathy.

Housand, B. C. (2018). *Fighting fake news!: Teaching critical thinking and media literacy in a digital age*. Prufrock Press.

Learning for Justice. (2019). *Learning for Justice Social Justice Anchor Standards*. The Southern Poverty Law Center.

Afterword

Lori Leibowitz

Lori Leibowitz was awarded the National Gifted Coordinator of the Year award in 2020 by the National Association of Gifted Children. She is currently a doctoral candidate at Baylor University School of Education. She is also the educational administrator for the gifted and talented program in Norwalk, Connecticut. She coordinates with twelve elementary schools and four middle schools to service high ability learners and their teachers. Lori is a fierce advocate for all students. Her leading charge has been the redesign of the gifted program to include more equitable identification practices, professional development for all staff members, and implementation of a culturally relevant curriculum. We couldn't think of a better person to write the afterword to our book, than our fearless leader and friend.

What comes next after completely transforming your gifted program from an isolated pull-out program for a few students to one that embraces a talent development approach with an emphasis on identifying students from historically underserved populations?

This is the question we faced after redesigning our gifted program almost four years ago. The idea was to open doors for students and raise the rigor in our work, so we immediately started brainstorming ideas of how to meet the needs of all students. Under the umbrella of the Schoolwide Enrichment Model and the guidance of Dr. Joseph Renzulli, its founder, the Norwalk Public School system completely overhauled its identification protocols. We moved to employ a universal nonverbal ability screener, used gifted behavior rating scales, assessed multiple data pieces, all while embracing a rolling admissions process. By offering a continuum of services, we were able to work with more students showing high potential than ever before. After just one identification window, our identified students increased by over 200. We had unlocked the gates and began to celebrate, but our work was just beginning.

The idea of a social justice curriculum just made sense. While the concept of social justice and multicultural curriculum had been studied in the past, primarily in urban school settings, it did not come without controversy. Some opponents of social justice in schools worry that the topics are too sensitive. Others argue that a social justice curriculum pushes particular political views on students. But the research was clear. Torres-Harding et al. (2018) explained that students engaged in projects with social justice focus could look for root causes of social problems, therefore, allowing them to become critical thinkers and agents of change. We knew we wanted our program to be student-centered and engaging, but the idea of passion projects just seemed safe and expected.

We became inspired by the work of *Learning for Justice,* formally known as *Teaching Tolerance.* We embraced the topics of identity, innovation, empathy, diversity, justice, and action and started designing curricular units and safe places for students to explore these topics. We encouraged our students to dig deep, question the status quo, and ask difficult questions. Most importantly, we believed in them and their ability to create change and dismantle systems of inequities facing them daily.

The results? They found their voices and never looked back. Our curriculum continues to evolve as we find new ways to empower our students, our future leaders. We encourage you to take the leap with social justice. When you give your students the tools and skills they need to become critical agents of change, the possibilities are endless.

Lori Leibowitz

References

Torres-Harding, S., Baber, A., Hilvers, J., Hobbs, N., & Maly, M. (2018). Children as agents of social and community change: Enhancing youth empowerment through participation in a school-based social activism project. *Education, Citizenship and Social Justice*, 13(1), 3–18. doi:10.1177/1746197916684643

Appendix A

Guest Speaker Letter Template

Dear _____,

In Gifted & Talented this year, we are investigating social justice issues based on student choice and interest. Students are empowered to ask questions about real-world issues. Grade ____ students are exploring a variety of topics in the hopes of making meaningful change in their community.

The students are studying_____
by investigating _____.
So far, they have_____.
They are curious to learn more about _____.

As an expert in the field of _____, we would love to invite you to speak on this topic. You are welcome to visit our classroom virtually or in-person depending on what's best for you.

If you are interested, please let me know.

Sincerely,

_____

Empowered Leaders: A Social Justice Curriculum for Gifted Learners

Appendix B

Name: _____ Date: _____

Choice Board

Directions: Choose _____ activities to complete. Write one paragraph detailing what you learned from these activities.

Read	Watch	Create
Watch	Analyze	Research
Explore	Watch	Read

_____
_____
_____

Empowered Leaders: A Social Justice Curriculum for Gifted Learners

Appendix C

Theme Project Assessment Rubric

	3	2	1
Restate the Question	Student restates the question, starting their essay clearly.	Student partially restates the question.	Student does not restate the question. Their essay does not start off clearly.
Answer the Question	Student answers the question fully.	Student partially answers the question.	Student does not answer the question.
Cite Evidence	Student cites multiple examples.	Student cites only one example.	Student does not cite any examples.
Explain Evidence	Student explains and/or expands on multiple examples.	Student explains and/or expands on only one example.	Student does not explain and/or expand on any examples.
Spelling & Grammar	Student clearly revised and edited their essay for clarity and style. There are fewer than three grammar mistakes present.	Student revised and edited their essay for clarity and style, but there are fewer than five grammar mistakes present.	Student did not revise and edit their essay for clarity and style. There are more than five grammar mistakes present.

Score

15 = 100   9 = 70
14 = 95   8 = 65
13 = 90   7 = 60
12 = 85   6 = 55
11 = 80   5 = 50

Student Name(s):

Comments:

Empowered Leaders: A Social Justice Curriculum for Gifted Learners

Appendix D

Theme Project Rubric

	20	15	10	5	0
Topic	Topic is clearly defined.	Topic is defined.	Topic is somewhat defined.	Topic is not clearly defined.	No topic.
Product	Product is relevant and very well done.	Product is relevant.	Product shows some effort.	Product demonstrates little effort.	No product.
Research	There are more than three reliable sources with complete notes.	There are three reliable sources with complete notes.	There are three reliable sources without complete notes.	There are fewer than three reliable sources without complete notes.	No sources.
Effort	Work completed above and beyond requirements.	Work completed fulfills all requirements.	Work completed.	Little demonstrated effort.	No demonstrated effort.
Connection to the Theme	Clearly connected to the theme.	Connected to the theme.	Somewhat connected to the theme.	Not clearly connected to the theme.	No connection.

Score: _____ /100

Student Name(s):

Comments:

Appendix E

Product Options

Here is a list of possible products you can create for your Theme Project. If you are interested in creating something else, ask your teacher for approval.

Arts & Music
Write a song
Perform a skit
Design a cartoon
Make a poster
Create a protest sign

Nature
Organize a park clean-up
Start a recycling program
Raise awareness about climate change
Compost at your school
Plant seeds

Community Service
Organize a fundraiser
Donate to a homeless shelter
Design a social media campaign
Rewrite a school policy
Plan a rally

Science & Math
Build a 3D model
Design an experiment
Make a graph
Create an infographic
Collect & Analyze data

Humanities
Write a poem or spoken word
Start writing a book
Design a children's book
Facilitate a book club
Write an essay

Technology
Record a podcast
Film a documentary
Build an app
Design a beat
Code a video game

Appendix F

Name: _____ Date: _____

Choice Board Worksheet

Directions: Write down your reactions after each choice board activity. Use the sentence starters below to guide your thoughts.

> Sentence Starters
> 1. I agree/disagree with the author because...
> 2. _____ connects to diversity because...
> 3. I felt _____ when I read _____ because...
> 4. One thing I noticed was....

Activity # _____   **Activity #** _____

Response: _____   Response: _____

_____   _____
_____   _____
_____   _____
_____   _____
_____   _____
_____   _____

Empowered Leaders: A Social Justice Curriculum for Gifted Learners

Appendix G

Name: _____ Date: _____

Choice Board Worksheet

Directions: Write down your reactions after each choice board activity. Use the sentence starters below to guide your thoughts.

```
Sentence Starters
1. I agree/disagree with the author because...
2. _____ connects to diversity because...
3. I felt _____ when I read _____ because...
4. One thing I noticed was....
```

Activity # _____

Response: _____
_____
_____

Activity # _____

Response: _____
_____
_____

Activity # _____

Response: _____
_____
_____

Appendix H

Enrichment Triad Model Examples

Here is a list of examples for each type of enrichment learning detailed in the Schoolwide Enrichment Model.

Type I Learning
Exploratory Activities

- Watch a video
- Invite in a guest speaker
- Explore a museum
- Read a book
- Listen to a podcast

Type II Learning
How To and Critical Thinking

- Learn a new skill
- Read a "how to" book
- Watch an instructional video
- Brainstorm ways to solve a problem

Type III Learning
Real World Investigations

- Organize a fundraiser
- Donate to a charity organization
- Rewrite a school policy
- Present to the Board of Education
- Facilitate a panel or discussion
- Start a recycling program